LAUDS

according to

the Benedictine Ritual

LATIN - ENGLISH

Copyright © Clear Creek Abbey, 2022
All Rights Reserved.
ISBN: 978-1-387-78387-8

Clearcreekmonks.org

Contents

SUNDAY - LAUDS 1
MONDAY - LAUDS 19
TUESDAY - LAUDS 33
WEDNESDAY - LAUDS 47
THURSDAY - LAUDS 61
FRIDAY - LAUDS 77
SATURDAY - LAUDS 93
CHAPTERS AND HYMNS FOR THE SEASONS 110
ADVENT 110
LENT 112
PASSIONTIDE 114
PASCHALTIDE 116

SUNDAY - LAUDS

℣. Deus in adiutórium meum inténde.

℟. Dómine, ad adiuvándum me festína. Glória Patri, et Fílio, * et Spirítui Sancto. Sicut erat in princípio, et nunc, et semper, * et in sǽcula sæculórum. Amen. Allelúia.

Psalmus 66

Deus misereátur nostri, et benedícat nobis: * illúminet vultum suum super nos, et misereátur nostri.

Ut cognoscámus in terra viam tuam, * in ómnibus géntibus salutáre tuum.

Confiteántur tibi pópuli, Deus: * confiteántur tibi pópuli omnes.

Læténtur et exsúltent gentes: † quóniam iúdicas pópulos in æquitáte, * et gentes in terra dírigis.

Confiteántur tibi pópuli, Deus, † confiteántur tibi pópuli omnes: * terra dedit fructum suum.

Benedícat nos Deus, Deus noster, benedícat nos Deus: * et métuant eum omnes fines terræ.

Glória Patri, et Fílio, * et Spirítui Sancto.

℣. O God, come to my assistance;

℟. O Lord, make haste to help me. Glory be to the Father, and to the Son, * and to the Holy Ghost. As it was in the beginning, is now, * and ever shall be, world without end. Amen. Alleluia.

Psalm 66

May God have mercy on us, and bless us: * may he cause the light of his countenance to shine upon us, and may he have mercy on us.

That we may know thy way upon earth: * thy salvation in all nations.

Let people confess to thee, O God: * let all people give praise to thee.

Let the nations be glad and rejoice: † for thou judgest the people with justice, * and directest the nations upon earth.

Let the people, O God, confess to thee: † let all the people give praise to thee: * the earth hath yielded her fruit.

May God, our God bless us, may God bless us: * and all the ends of the earth fear him.

Glory be to the Father, and to the Son, * and to the Holy Ghost.

Sunday - Lauds

Sicut erat in princípio, et nunc, et semper, * et in sǽcula sæculórum. Amen.	As it was in the beginning, is now, * and ever shall be, world without end. Amen.

On Sundays during the year, Psalms 50, 117, and 62 are said under the antiphon Alleluia, alleluia.

On Sundays during Paschaltide, Psalms 92, 99, and 62 are said under the antiphon Alleluia (x9)—go to page 6.

On Feast days the antiphons are proper and the Paschaltide psalms are used.

Antiphona in Dominicis per annum. Allelúia, † allelúia.	*Sundays during the year, Ant.* Alleluia † alleluia.
Psalmus 50 [1]	**Psalm 50 [1]**

MISERÉRE mei, Deus, * secúndum magnam misericórdiam tuam.

Et secúndum multitúdinem miseratiónum tuárum, * dele iniquitátem meam.

Amplius lava me ab iniquitáte mea: * et a peccáto meo munda me.

Quóniam iniquitátem meam ego cognósco: * et peccátum meum contra me est semper.

Tibi soli peccávi, et malum coram te feci: * ut iustificéris in sermónibus tuis, et vincas cum iudicáris.

Ecce enim, in iniquitátibus concéptus sum: * et in peccátis concépit me mater mea.

Ecce enim, veritátem dilexísti: * incérta et occúlta sapiéntiæ tuæ manifestásti mihi.

Aspérges me hyssópo, et mundábor: * lavábis me, et super nivem dealbábor.

HAVE mercy on me, O God, * according to thy great mercy.

And according to the multitude of thy tender mercies * blot out my iniquity.

Wash me yet more from my iniquity, * and cleanse me from my sin.

For I know my iniquity, * and my sin is always before me.

To thee only have I sinned, and have done evil before thee: * that thou mayst be justified in thy words, and mayst overcome when thou art judged.

For behold I was conceived in iniquities; * and in sins did my mother conceive me.

For behold thou hast loved truth: * the uncertain and hidden things of thy wisdom thou hast made manifest to me.

Thou shalt sprinkle me with hyssop, and I shall be cleansed: * thou shalt wash me, and I shall be made whiter than snow.

Sunday - Lauds

Audítui meo dabis gáudium et lætítiam: * et exsultábunt ossa humiliáta.

Avérte fáciem tuam a peccátis meis: * et omnes iniquitátes meas dele.

Cor mundum crea in me, Deus: * et spíritum rectum ínnova in viscéribus meis.

Ne proícias me a fácie tua: * et spíritum sanctum tuum ne áuferas a me.

Redde mihi lætítiam salutáris tui: * et spíritu principáli confírma me.

Docébo iníquos vias tuas: * et ímpii ad te converténtur.

Líbera me de sanguínibus, Deus, Deus salútis meæ: * et exsultábit lingua mea iustítiam tuam.

Dómine, lábia mea apéries: * et os meum annuntiábit laudem tuam.

Quóniam si voluísses sacrifícium, dedíssem útique: * holocáustis non delectáberis.

Sacrifícium Deo spíritus contribulátus: * cor contrítum, et humiliátum, Deus, non despícies.

Benígne fac, Dómine, in bona voluntáte tua Sion: * ut ædificéntur muri Ierúsalem.

Tunc acceptábis sacrifícium iustítiæ, oblatiónes, et holocáusta:

To my hearing thou shalt give joy and gladness: * and the bones that have been humbled shall rejoice.

Turn away thy face from my sins, * and blot out all my iniquities.

Create a clean heart in me, O God: * and renew a right spirit within my bowels.

Cast me not away from thy face; * and take not thy holy spirit from me.

Restore unto me the joy of thy salvation, * and strengthen me with a perfect spirit.

I will teach the unjust thy ways: * and the wicked shall be converted to thee.

Deliver me from blood, O God, thou God of my salvation: * and my tongue shall extol thy justice.

O Lord, thou wilt open my lips: * and my mouth shall declare thy praise.

For if thou hadst desired sacrifice, I would indeed have given it: * with burnt offerings thou wilt not be delighted.

A sacrifice to God is an afflicted spirit: * a contrite and humbled heart, O God, thou wilt not despise.

Deal favourably, O Lord, in thy good will with Sion; * that the walls of Jerusalem may be built up.

Then shalt thou accept the sacrifice of justice, oblations and whole burnt offerings: * then

Sunday - Lauds

* tunc impónent super altáre tuum vítulos.

Psalmus 117 [2]

CONFITÉMINI Dómino quóniam bonus: * quóniam in sǽculum misericórdia eius.

Dicat nunc Israël quóniam bonus: * quóniam in sǽculum misericórdia eius.

Dicat nunc domus Aaron: * quóniam in sǽculum misericórdia eius.

Dicant nunc qui timent Dóminum: * quóniam in sǽculum misericórdia eius.

De tribulatióne invocávi Dóminum: * et exaudívit me in latitúdine Dóminus.

Dóminus mihi adiútor: * non timébo quid fáciat mihi homo.

Dóminus mihi adiútor: * et ego despíciam inimícos meos.

Bonum est confídere in Dómino, * quam confídere in hómine:

Bonum est speráre in Dómino, * quam speráre in princípibus.

Omnes gentes circuiérunt me: * et in nómine Dómini quia ultus sum in eos.

Circumdántes circumdedérunt me: * et in nómine Dómini quia ultus sum in eos.

Circumdedérunt me sicut apes, † et exarsérunt sicut ignis in spinis: * et in nómine Dómini quia ultus sum in eos.

shall they lay calves upon thy altar.

Psalm 117 [2]

GIVE praise to the Lord, for he is good: * for his mercy endureth for ever.

Let Israel now say, that he is good: * that his mercy endureth for ever.

Let the house of Aaron now say, * that his mercy endureth for ever.

Let them that fear the Lord now say, * that his mercy endureth for ever.

In my trouble I called upon the Lord: * and the Lord heard me, and enlarged me.

The Lord is my helper: * I will not fear what man can do unto me.

The Lord is my helper: * and I will look over my enemies.

It is good to confide in the Lord, * rather than to have confidence in man.

It is good to trust in the Lord, * rather than to trust in princes.

All nations compassed me about; * and in the name of the Lord I have been revenged on them.

Surrounding me they compassed me about: * and in the name of the Lord I have been revenged on them.

They surrounded me like bees, † and they burned like fire among thorns: * and in the name of the Lord I was revenged on them.

Sunday - Lauds

Impúlsus evérsus sum ut cáderem: * et Dóminus suscépit me.

Fortitúdo mea, et laus mea Dóminus: * et factus est mihi in salútem.

Vox exsultatiónis, et salútis * in tabernáculis iustórum.

Déxtera Dómini fecit virtútem: † déxtera Dómini exaltávit me, * déxtera Dómini fecit virtútem.

Non móriar, sed vivam: * et narrábo ópera Dómini.

Castígans castigávit me Dóminus: * et morti non trádidit me.

Aperíte mihi portas iustítiæ, † ingréssus in eas confitébor Dómino: * hæc porta Dómini, iusti intrábunt in eam.

Confitébor tibi quóniam exaudísti me: * et factus es mihi in salútem.

Lápidem, quem reprobavérunt ædificántes: * hic factus est in caput ánguli.

A Dómino factum est istud: * et est mirábile in óculis nostris.

Hæc est dies, quam fecit Dóminus: * exsultémus, et lætémur in ea.

O Dómine, salvum me fac, † o Dómine, bene prosperáre: * benedíctus qui venit in nómine Dómini.

Being pushed I was overturned that I might fall: * but the Lord supported me.

The Lord is my strength and my praise: * and he is become my salvation.

The voice of rejoicing and of salvation * is in the tabernacles of the just.

The right hand of the Lord hath wrought strength: † the right hand of the Lord hath exalted me: * the right hand of the Lord hath wrought strength.

I shall not die, but live: * and shall declare the works of the Lord.

The Lord chastising hath chastised me: * but he hath not delivered me over to death.

Open ye to me the gates of justice: † I will go in to them, and give praise to the Lord. * This is the gate of the Lord, the just shall enter into it.

I will give glory to thee because thou hast heard me: * and art become my salvation.

The stone which the builders rejected; * the same is become the head of the corner.

This is the Lord's doing: * and it is wonderful in our eyes.

This is the day which the Lord hath made: * let us be glad and rejoice therein.

O Lord, save me: † O Lord, give good success: * Blessed be he that cometh in the name of the Lord.

Sunday - Lauds

Benedíximus vobis de domo Dómini: * Deus Dóminus, et illúxit nobis.

Constitúite diem solémnem in condénsis, * usque ad cornu altáris.

Deus meus es tu, et confitébor tibi: * Deus meus es tu, et exaltábo te.

Confitébor tibi quóniam exaudísti me * et factus es mihi in salútem.

Confitémini Dómino quóniam bonus: * quóniam in sǽculum misericórdia eius.

We have blessed you out of the house of the Lord: * The Lord is God, and he hath shone upon us.

Appoint a solemn day, with shady boughs, * even to the horn of the altar.

Thou art my God, and I will praise thee: * thou art my God, and I will exalt thee.

I will praise thee, because thou hast heard me, * and art become my salvation.

O praise ye the Lord, for he is good: * for his mercy endureth for ever.

On Sundays during the year, skip to Psalm 62.

On Sundays during Paschaltide, the preceding two psalms are replaced by the following two: Psalms 92, 99, and 62 are said under the antiphon Alleluia (x9).

On Feast days the antiphons are proper and the Paschaltide psalms are used (92, 99, and 62).

In Dominicis temporis paschalis, Ant. Allelúia, † allelúia, allelúia; Allelúia, allelúia, allelúia; Allelúia, allelúia, allelúia.

On Sundays in Paschaltide, Ant. Alleluia, † alleluia, alleluia; Alleluia, alleluia, alleluia; Alleluia, alleluia, alleluia.

Psalmus 92 [1]

Dóminus regnávit, decórem indútus est: * indútus est Dóminus fortitúdinem, et præcínxit se.

Etenim firmávit orbem terræ, * qui non commovébitur.

Paráta sedes tua ex tunc: * a sǽculo tu es.

Psalm 92 [1]

The Lord hath reigned, he is clothed with beauty: * the Lord is clothed with strength, and hath girded himself.

For he hath established the world * which shall not be moved.

Thy throne is prepared from of old: * thou art from everlasting.

Sunday - Lauds

Elevavérunt flúmina, Dómine: * elevavérunt flúmina vocem suam.

Elevavérunt flúmina fluctus suos, * a vócibus aquárum multárum.

Mirábiles elatiónes maris: * mirábilis in altis Dóminus.

Testimónia tua credibília facta sunt nimis: * domum tuam decet sanctitúdo, Dómine, in longitúdinem diérum.

Psalmus 99 [2]

Iubiláte Deo, omnis terra: * servíte Dómino in lætítia.

Introíte in conspéctu eius, * in exsultatióne.

Scitóte quóniam Dóminus ipse est Deus: * ipse fecit nos, et non ipsi nos.

Pópulus eius, et oves páscuæ eius: † introíte portas eius in confessióne, * átria eius in hymnis: confitémini illi.

Laudáte nomen eius: quóniam suávis est Dóminus, † in ætérnum misericórdia eius, * et usque in generatiónem et generatiónem véritas eius.

Psalmus 62 [3]

Deus, Deus meus, * ad te de luce vígilo.

Sitívit in te ánima mea, * quam multíplíciter tibi caro mea.

The floods have lifted up, O Lord: * the floods have lifted up their voice.

The floods have lifted up their waves, * with the noise of many waters.

Wonderful are the surges of the sea: * wonderful is the Lord on high.

Thy testimonies are become exceedingly credible: * holiness becometh thy house, O Lord, unto length of days.

Psalm 99 [2]

Sing joyfully to God, all the earth: * serve ye the Lord with gladness.

Come in before his presence * with exceeding great joy.

Know ye that the Lord he is God: * he made us, and not we ourselves.

We are his people and the sheep of his pasture. † Go ye into his gates with praise, * into his courts with hymns: and give glory to him.

Praise ye his name: for the Lord is sweet, † his mercy endureth for ever, * and his truth to generation and generation.

Psalm 62 [3]

O God, my God, * to thee do I watch at break of day.

For thee my soul hath thirsted; * for thee my flesh, O how many ways!

Sunday - Lauds

In terra desérta, et ínvia, et inaquósa: † sic in sancto appárui tibi, * ut vidérem virtútem tuam, et glóriam tuam.

Quóniam mélior est misericórdia tua super vitas: * lábia mea laudábunt te.

Sic benedícam te in vita mea: * et in nómine tuo levábo manus meas.

Sicut ádipe et pinguédine repleátur ánima mea: * et lábiis exsultatiónis laudábit os meum.

Si memor fui tui super stratum meum, † in matutínis meditábor in te: * quia fuísti adiútor meus.

Et in velaménto alárum tuárum exsultábo, † adhǽsit ánima mea post te: * me suscépit déxtera tua.

Ipsi vero in vanum quæsiérunt ánimam meam, † introíbunt in inferióra terræ: * tradéntur in manus gládii, partes vúlpium erunt.

Rex vero lætábitur in Deo, † laudabúntur omnes qui iurant in eo: * quia obstrúctum est os loquéntium iníqua.

In Dominicis Per annum, Ant. Allelúia, allelúia.

Ant. Tres púeri † iussu régis in fornácem missi sunt, non timéntes flammam ignis dicéntes: Benedíctus Deus.

In a desert land, and where there is no way, and no water: † so in the sanctuary have I come before thee, * to see thy power and thy glory.

For thy mercy is better than lives: * thee my lips shall praise.

Thus will I bless thee all my life long: * and in thy name I will lift up my hands.

Let my soul be filled as with marrow and fatness: * and my mouth shall praise thee with joyful lips.

If I have remembered thee upon my bed, † I will meditate on thee in the morning: * because thou hast been my helper.

And I will rejoice under the covert of thy wings: † my soul hath stuck close to thee: * thy right hand hath received me.

But they have sought my soul in vain, † they shall go into the lower parts of the earth: * they shall be delivered into the hands of the sword, they shall be the portions of foxes.

But the king shall rejoice in God, † all they shall be praised that swear by him: * because the mouth is stopped of them that speak wicked things.

Sundays during the year, Ant. Alleluia, alleluia.

Ant. The three young boys † cast into the furnace by the king, fearing not the flames of fire, said: Blessed be God.

In Dominicis temporis paschalis, Ant. Allelúia, allelúia, allelúia; Allelúia, allelúia, allelúia; Allelúia, allelúia, allelúia.

Ant. Surréxit Christus † de sepúlcro, qui liberávit tres púeros de camíno ignis ardéntis, allelúia.

Canticum Trium Puerorum [4]

Dan. 3:57-88,56

Benedícite, ómnia ópera Dómini, Dómino: * laudáte et superexaltáte eum in sǽcula.

Benedícite, Angeli Dómini, Dómino: * benedícite, cæli, Dómino.

Benedícite, aquæ omnes, quæ super cælos sunt, Dómino: * benedícite, omnes virtútes Dómini, Dómino.

Benedícite, sol et luna, Dómino: * benedícite, stellæ cæli, Dómino.

Benedícite, omnis imbcr ct ros, Dómino: * benedícite, omnes spíritus Dei, Dómino.

Benedícite, ignis et æstus, Dómino: * benedícite, frigus et æstus, Dómino.

Benedícite, rores et pruína, Dómino: * benedícite, gelu et frigus, Dómino.

Benedícite, glácies et nives, Dómino: * benedícite, noctes et dies, Dómino.

Benedícite, lux et ténebræ, Dómino: * benedícite, fúlgura et nubes, Dómino.

On Sundays in Paschaltide, Ant. Alleluia, alleluia, alleluia; Alleluia, alleluia, alleluia; Alleluia, alleluia, alleluia.

Ant. Risen is Christ † from the grave, who freed the three young men from the burning furnace of fire, alleluia.

Canticle of the Three Young Men [4]

Dan. 3:57-88,56

All ye works of the Lord, bless the Lord: * praise and exalt him above all for ever.

O ye angels of the Lord, bless the Lord: * O ye heavens, bless the Lord:

O all ye waters that are above the heavens, bless the Lord: * O all ye powers of the Lord, bless the Lord.

O ye sun and moon, bless the Lord: * O ye stars of heaven, bless the Lord.

O every shower and dew, bless ye the Lord: * O all ye spirits of God, bless the Lord.

O ye fire and heat, bless the Lord: * O ye cold and heat, bless the Lord.

O ye dews and hoar frosts, bless the Lord: * O ye frost and cold, bless the Lord.

O ye ice and snow, bless the Lord: * O ye nights and days, bless the Lord.

O ye light and darkness, bless the Lord: * O ye lightnings and clouds, bless the Lord.

10   *Sunday - Lauds*

Benedícat terra Dóminum: * laudet et superexáltet eum in sǽcula.

Benedícite, montes et colles, Dómino: * benedícite, univérsa germinántia in terra, Dómino.

Benedícite, fontes, Dómino: * benedícite, mária et flúmina, Dómino.

Benedícite, cete, et ómnia, quæ movéntur in aquis, Dómino: * benedícite, omnes vólucres cæli, Dómino.

Benedícite, omnes béstiæ et pécora, Dómino: * benedícite, fílii hóminum, Dómino.

Benedícat Israël Dóminum: * laudet et superexáltet eum in sǽcula.

Benedícite, sacerdótes Dómini, Dómino: * benedícite, servi Dómini, Dómino.

Benedícite, spíritus, et ánimæ iustórum, Dómino: * benedícite, sancti, et húmiles corde, Dómino.

Benedícite, Ananía, Azaría, Mísaël, Dómino: * laudáte et superexaltáte eum in sǽcula.

(Fit reverentia:) Benedicámus Patrem et Fílium cum Sancto Spíritu: * laudémus et superexaltémus eum in sǽcula.

Benedíctus es, Dómine, in firmaménto cæli: * et laudábilis, et gloriósus, et superexaltátus in sǽcula.

Hic non dicitur Gloria Patri, neque Amen.

O let the earth bless the Lord: * let it praise and exalt him above all for ever.

O ye mountains and hills, bless the Lord: * O all ye things that spring up in the earth, bless the Lord.

O ye fountains, bless the Lord: * O ye seas and rivers, bless the Lord.

O ye whales, and all that move in the waters, bless the Lord: * O all ye fowls of the air, bless the Lord.

O all ye beasts and cattle, bless the Lord: * O ye sons of men, bless the Lord.

O let Israel bless the Lord: * let them praise and exalt him above all for ever.

O ye priests of the Lord, bless the Lord: * O ye servants of the Lord, bless the Lord.

O ye spirits and souls of the just, bless the Lord: * O ye holy and humble of heart, bless the Lord.

O Ananias, Azarias, and Misael, bless ye the Lord: * praise and exalt him above all for ever.

(Reverence is made:) Let us bless the Father and the Son, with the Holy Ghost; * let us praise and exalt him above all for ever.

Blessed art thou, O Lord, in the firmament of heaven: * and worthy of praise, and glorious for ever.

Here neither the Glory be, nor the Amen is said.

Sunday - Lauds

In Dominicis per annum, Ant.
Tres púeri iussu régis in fornácem missi sunt, non timéntes flammam ignis dicéntes: Benedíctus Deus.
Ant. Allelúia, † allelúia, allelúia.

In Dominicis temporis paschalis, Ant. Surréxit Christus de sepúlcro, qui liberávit tres púeros de camíno ignis ardéntis, allelúia.

Ant. Allelúia, † allelúia, allelúia.

Psalmus 148 [5]

LAUDÁTE Dóminum de cælis: * laudáte eum in excélsis.

Laudáte eum, omnes Angeli eius: * laudáte eum, omnes virtútes eius.

Laudáte eum, sol et luna: * laudáte eum, omnes stellæ et lumen.

Laudáte eum, cæli cælórum: * et aquæ omnes, quæ super cælos sunt, laudent nomen Dómini.

Quia ipse dixit, et facta sunt: * ipse mandávit, et creáta sunt.

Státuit ea in ætérnum, et in sǽculum sǽculi: * præcéptum pósuit, et non prætéribit.

Laudáte Dóminum de terra, * dracónes, et omnes abýssi.

Ignis, grando, nix, glácies, spíritus procellárum: * quæ fáciunt verbum eius:

Sundays during the year, Ant.
The three young boys cast into the furnace by the king, fearing not the flames of fire, said: Blessed be God.
Ant. Alleluia, † alleluia, alleluia.

On Sundays in Paschaltide, Ant. Risen is Christ from the grave, who freed the three young men from the burning furnace of fire, alleluia.

Ant. Alleluia, † alleluia, alleluia.

Psalm 148 [5]

PRAISE ye the Lord from the heavens * praise ye him in the high places.

Praise ye him, all his angels: * praise ye him, all his hosts.

Praise ye him, O sun and moon: * praise him, all ye stars and light.

Praise him, ye heavens of heavens: * and let all the waters that are above the heavens, praise the name of the Lord.

For he spoke, and they were made: * he commanded, and they were created.

He hath established them for ever, and for ages of ages: * he hath made a decree, and it shall not pass away.

Praise the Lord from the earth, * ye dragons, and all ye deeps:

Fire, hail, snow, ice, stormy winds * which fulfill his word:

Sunday - Lauds

Montes, et omnes colles: * ligna fructífera, et omnes cedri.

Béstiæ, et univérsa pécora: * serpéntes, et vólucres pennátæ:

Reges terræ, et omnes pópuli: * príncipes, et omnes iúdices terræ.

Iúvenes, et vírgines: † senes cum iunióribus laudent nomen Dómini: * quia exaltátum est nomen eius solíus.

Conféssio eius super cælum et terram: * et exaltávit cornu pópuli sui.

Hymnus ómnibus sanctis eius: * fíliis Israël, pópulo appropinquánti sibi.

Hic non dicitur Gloria Patri.

Psalmus 149 [6]

CANTÁTE Dómino cánticum novum: * laus eius in ecclésia sanctórum.

Lætétur Israël in eo, qui fecit eum: * et fílii Sion exsúltent in rege suo.

Laudent nomen eius in choro: * in týmpano, et psaltério psallant ei:

Quia beneplácitum est Dómino in pópulo suo: * et exaltábit mansuétos in salútem.

Exsultábunt sancti in glória: * lætabúntur in cubílibus suis.

Exaltatiónes Dei in gútture eórum: * et gládii ancípites in mánibus eórum.

Ad faciéndam vindíctam in natiónibus: * increpatiónes in pópulis.

Mountains and all hills, * fruitful trees and all cedars:

Beasts and all cattle: * serpents and feathered fowls:

Kings of the earth and all people: * princes and all judges of the earth:

Young men and maidens: † let the old with the younger, praise the name of the Lord: * For his name alone is exalted.

The praise of him is above heaven and earth: * and he hath exalted the horn of his people.

A hymn to all his saints: to the children of Israel, a people approaching him.

Here the Glory be is not said.

Psalm 149 [6]

SING ye to the Lord a new canticle: * let his praise be in the church of the saints.

Let Israel rejoice in him that made him: * and let the children of Sion be joyful in their king.

Let them praise his name in choir: * let them sing to him with the timbrel and the psaltery.

For the Lord is well pleased with his people: * and he will exalt the meek unto salvation.

The saints shall rejoice in glory: * they shall be joyful in their beds.

The high praises of God shall be in their mouth: * and two-edged swords in their hands:

To execute vengeance upon the nations, * chastisements among the people:

Sunday - Lauds

Ad alligándos reges eórum in compédibus: * et nóbiles eórum in mánicis férreis.

Ut fáciant in eis iudícium conscríptum: * glória hæc est ómnibus sanctis eius.

Hic non dicitur Gloria Patri.

Psalmus 150 [7]

Laudáte Dóminum in sanctis eius: * laudáte eum in firmaménto virtútis eius.

Laudáte eum in virtútibus eius: * laudáte eum secúndum multitúdinem magnitúdinis eius.

Laudáte eum in sono tubæ: * laudáte eum in psaltério, et cíthara.

Laudáte eum in týmpano, et choro: * laudáte eum in chordis, et órgano.

Laudáte eum in cýmbalis benesonántibus: † laudáte eum in cýmbalis iubilatiónis: * omnis spíritus laudet Dóminum.

Glória Patri, et Fílio, * et Spirítui Sancto.

Sicut erat in princípio, et nunc, et semper, * et in sǽcula sæculórum. Amen.

In Dominicis per annum et tempore paschali: Ant. Allelúia, allelúia, allelúia.

Capitulum   *Apoc. 7:12*

BENEDÍCTIO, et cláritas, et sapiéntia, et gratiárum áctio, † honor, virtus, et fortitúdo Deo nostro * in sǽcula sæculórum. Amen.

℟. Deo grátias.

To bind their kings with fetters, * and their nobles with manacles of iron.

To execute upon them the judgment that is written: * this glory is to all his saints.

Here the Glory be is not said.

Psalm 150 [7]

PRAISE ye the Lord in his holy places: * praise ye him in the firmament of his power.

Praise ye him for his mighty acts: * praise ye him according to the multitude of his greatness.

Praise him with sound of trumpet: * praise him with psaltery and harp.

Praise him with timbrel and choir: * praise him with strings and organs.

Praise him on high sounding cymbals: † praise him on cymbals of joy: * let every spirit praise the Lord.

Glory be to the Father, and to the Son, * and to the Holy Ghost.

As it was in the beginning, is now, * and ever shall be, world without end. Amen.

On Sundays during the year and in Paschaltide, Ant. Alleluia alleluia, alleluia.

Chapter   *Rev. 7:12*

BENEDICTION, and glory, and wisdom, and thanksgiving, † honour, and power, and strength to our God * for ever and ever. Amen.

℟. Thanks be to God.

Sunday - Lauds

℟.br. Inclína cor meum, Deus, * In testimónia tua.

℟. Inclína cor meum, Deus, * In testimónia tua.

℣. Avérte óculos meos, ne vídeant vanitátem: in via tua vivífica me.

℟. In testimónia tua.

℣. Glória Patri, et Fílio, * et Spirítui Sancto.

℟. Inclína cor meum, Deus, * in testimónia tua.

Sequens Hymnus dicitur in Dominicis post Epiphaniam a die 14 Januarii usque ad Dominicam Quinquagesimæ inclusive, et a Dominica proximiori Kalendis Octobris, scilicet a die 28 Septembris, usque ad Dominicam ultimam post Pentecosten.

Hymnus

Ætérne rerum Cónditor,
Noctem diémque qui regis,
Et témporum das témpora,
Ut álleves fastídium.

Præco diéi iam sonat,
Noctis profúndæ pérvigil,
Noctúrna lux viántibus,
A nocte noctem ségregans.

Hoc excitátus Lúcifer
Solvit polum calígine,
Hoc omnis errónum cohors
Viam nocéndi déserit.

Hoc nauta vires cólligit,
Pontíque mitéscunt freta:

℟.br. Incline my heart * into thy testimonies.

℟. Incline my heart * into thy testimonies.

℣. Turn away my eyes that they may not behold vanity: quicken me in thy way.

℟. Into thy testimonies.

℣. Glory be to the Father, and to the Son, * and to the Holy Ghost.

℟. Incline my heart * into thy testimonies.

The following hymn is said on the Sundays after Epiphany from January 14 until Quinquagesima Sunday inclusive, and from the Sunday closest to October 1, namely from September 28, until the last Sunday after Pentecost.

Hymn

Maker of all, eternal King,
Who day and night about dost bring:
Who weary mortals to relieve,
Dost in their times the seasons give:

Now the shrill cock proclaims the day,
And calls the sun's awak'ning ray
The wand'ring pilgrim's guiding light,
That marks the watches night by night.

Roused at the note, the morning star
Heaven's dusky veil uplifts afar:
Night's vagrant bands no longer roam,
But from their dark ways hie them home.

The encouraged sailor's fears are o'er,
The foaming billows rage no more:

Sunday - Lauds

Hoc, ipsa Petra Ecclésiæ,
Canénte, culpam díluit.

Surgámus ergo strénue,
Gallus iacéntes éxcitat,
Et somnoléntos íncrepat,
Gallus negántes árguit.

Gallo canénte spes redit,
Ægris salus refúnditur,
Mucro latrónis cónditur,
Lapsis fides revértitur.

Iesu labéntes réspice,
Et nos vidéndo córrige:
Si réspicis, lapsus cadunt,
Fletúque culpa sólvitur.

Tu lux refúlge sénsibus,
Mentísque somnum díscute:
Te nostra vox primum sonet,
Et vota solvámus tibi.

Deo Patri sit glória,
Eiúsque soli Fílio,
Cum Spíritu Paráclito,
Et nunc et in perpétuum.
Amen.

Lo! e'en the very Church's rock
Melts at the crowing of the cock.

O let us then like men arise;
The cock rebukes our slumbering eyes,
Bestirs who still in sleep would lie,
And shames who would their Lord deny.

New hope his clarion-note awakes,
Sickness the feeble frame forsakes,
The robber sheathes his lawless sword,
Faith to the fallen is restored.

Look on us, Jesu, when we fall,
And with thy look our souls recall:
If thou but look, our sins are gone,
And with due tears our pardon won.

Shed through our hearts thy piercing ray,
Our souls' dull slumber drive away:
Thy name be first on every tongue,
To thee our earliest praises sung.

All laud to God the Father be,
All praise, Eternal Son, to thee,
All glory, as is ever meet,
To God the holy Paraclete.
Amen.

Sequens Hymnus dicitur in Dominica II et reliquis Dominicis post Pentecosten usque ad Dominicam proximiorem Kalendis Octobris, id est ad diem 27 Septembris inclusive occurrentibus.

Hymnus

Ecce iam noctis tenuátur umbra,
Lucis auróra rútilans corúscat:

The following Hymn is said on the second and the rest of the Sundays after Pentecost until the Sunday closest to October 1, that is until September 27, inclusive.

Hymn

Lo, the dim shadows of the night are waning;
Lightsome and blushing, dawn of day returneth;
Fervent in spirit, to the world's

16 Sunday - Lauds

Nísibus totis rogitémus omnes
Cunctipoténtem:

Ut Deus nostri miserátus, omnem
Pellat languórem, tríbuat salútem,
Donet et nobis pietáte Patris
Regna polorum.

Præstet hoc nobis Déitas beáta
Pátris, ac Nati, paritérque Sancti
Spíritus, cuius réboat in omni
Glória mundo.
Amen.

℣. Dóminus regnávit, decórem
índuit.
℟. Induit Dóminus fortitúdinem, et præcínxit se virtúte.

Canticum Zachariæ
Luc. 1:68-79

BENEDÍCTUS ✠ Dóminus, Deus
Israël: * quia visitávit, et
fecit redemptiónem plebis suæ:

Et eréxit cornu salútis nobis: *
in domo David, púeri sui.

Sicut locútus est per os
sanctórum, * qui a sǽculo sunt,
prophetárum eius:
Salútem ex inimícis nostris, *
et de manu ómnium, qui odérunt
nos.
Ad faciéndam misericórdiam
cum pátribus nostris: * et memorári testaménti sui sancti.

Creator
Pray we devoutly:

That he may pity sinners in their sighing,
Banish all troubles, kindly health
bestowing;
And may he grant us, of his countless
blessings,
Peace that is endless.

This be our portion, God forever blessed,
Father eternal, Son, and Holy Spirit,
Whose is the glory, which through all
creation
Ever resoundeth. Amen.

℣ The Lord reigns, he is clothed
with beauty.
℟. The Lord is clothed with
strength, and has girded himself.

Canticle of Zacharias
Luke 1:68-79

Blessed be the Lord ✠ God of
Israel; * because he hath visited
and wrought the redemption of
his people:

And hath raised up an horn of
salvation to us, * in the house of
David his servant:

As he spoke by the mouth of
his holy Prophets, * who are from
the beginning:
Salvation from our enemies, *
and from the hand of all that hate
us:
To perform mercy to our fathers, * and to remember his holy
testament,

Sunday - Lauds

Iusiurándum, quod iurávit ad Abraham patrem nostrum, * datúrum se nobis:

Ut sine timóre, de manu inimicórum nostrórum liberáti, * serviámus illi.

In sanctitáte, et iustítia coram ipso, * ómnibus diébus nostris.

Et tu, puer, Prophéta Altíssimi vocáberis: * præíbis enim ante fáciem Dómini, paráre vias eius:

Ad dandam sciéntiam salútis plebi eius: * in remissiónem peccatórum eórum:

Per víscera misericórdiæ Dei nostri: * in quibus visitávit nos, óriens ex alto:

Illumináre his, qui in ténebris, et in umbra mortis sedent: * ad dirigéndos pedes nostros in viam pacis.

Kýrie, eléison. Christe, eléison. Kýrie, eléison.

Pater noster, qui es in cælis, sanctificétur nomen tuum: advéniat regnum tuum: fiat volúntas tua, sicut in cælo et in terra. Panem nostrum cotidiánum da nobis hódie: et dimítte nobis débita nostra, sicut et nos dimíttimus debitóribus nostris:

℣. Et ne nos indúcas in tentatiónem:

℟. Sed líbera nos a malo.

℣. Dóminus vobíscum.

℟. Et cum spíritu tuo.

℣. Benedicámus Dómino.

The oath, which he swore to Abraham our father, * that he would grant to us,

That being delivered from the hand of our enemies, * we may serve him without fear,

In holiness and justice before him, * all our days.

And thou, child, shalt be called the prophet of the Highest: * for thou shalt go before the face of the Lord to prepare his ways:

To give knowledge of salvation to his people, * unto the remission of their sins:

Through the bowels of the mercy of our God, * in which the Orient from on high hath visited us:

To enlighten them that sit in darkness, and in the shadow of death: * to direct our feet into the way of peace.

Lord have mercy upon us, Christ have mercy upon us, Lord have mercy upon us

Our Father, who art in heaven, Hallowed be thy name. Thy kingdom come. Thy will be done on earth as it is in heaven. Give us this day our daily bread. And forgive us our trespasses, as we forgive those who trespass against us.

℣. And lead us not into temptation:

℟. But deliver us from evil.

℣. The Lord be with you.

℟. And with your spirit.

℣. Let us bless the Lord.

℟. Deo grátias.
℣. Fidélium ánimæ per misericórdiam Dei requiéscant in pace.
℟. Amen.
℣. Divínum auxílium máneat semper nobíscum.
℟. Et cum frátribus nostris abséntibus. Amen.

℟. Thanks be to God.
℣. May the souls of the faithful, through the mercy of God, rest in peace.
℟. Amen.
℣. May the divine assistance remain with us always.
℟. And with our brothers, who are absent. Amen.

MONDAY - LAUDS

℣. Deus in adiutórium meum inténde.

℞. Dómine, ad adiuvándum me festína. Glória Patri, et Fílio, * et Spirítui Sancto. Sicut erat in princípio, et nunc, et semper, * et in sǽcula sæculórum. Amen. Allelúia.

Psalmus 66

DEUS misereátur nostri, et benedícat nobis: * illúminet vultum suum super nos, et misereátur nostri.

Ut cognoscámus in terra viam tuam, * in ómnibus géntibus salutáre tuum.
Confiteántur tibi pópuli, Deus: * confiteántur tibi pópuli omnes.

Læténtur et exsúltent gentes: † quóniam iúdicas pópulos in æquitáte, * et gentes in terra dírigis.
Confiteántur tibi pópuli, Deus, † confiteántur tibi pópuli omnes: * terra dedit fructum suum.

Benedícat nos Deus, Deus noster, benedícat nos Deus: * et métuant eum omnes fines terræ.
Glória Patri, et Fílio, * et Spirítui Sancto.

℣. O God, come to my assistance;

℞. O Lord, make haste to help me. Glory be to the Father, and to the Son, * and to the Holy Ghost. As it was in the beginning, is now, * and ever shall be, world without end. Amen. Alleluia.

Psalm 66

MAY God have mercy on us, and bless us: * may he cause the light of his countenance to shine upon us, and may he have mercy on us.

That we may know thy way upon earth: * thy salvation in all nations.
Let people confess to thee, O God: * let all people give praise to thee.

Let the nations be glad and rejoice: † for thou judgest the people with justice, * and directest the nations upon earth.
Let the people, O God, confess to thee: † let all the people give praise to thee: * the earth hath yielded her fruit.

May God, our God bless us, may God bless us: * and all the ends of the earth fear him.
Glory be to the Father, and to the Son, * and to the Holy Ghost.

Sicut erat in princípio, et nunc, et semper, * et in sǽcula sæculórum. Amen.

Per annum, Ant. Miserére † mei, Deus.

Et non repetitur in psalmo.

Tempore paschali, Ant. Allelúia, † allelúia, allelúia.

Et dicitur tres psalmi sequentes sub una antiphona.

Psalmus 50 [1]

Miserére mei, Deus, * secúndum magnam misericórdiam tuam.

Et secúndum multitúdinem miseratiónum tuárum, * dele iniquitátem meam.

Amplius lava me ab iniquitáte mea: * et a peccáto meo munda me.

Quóniam iniquitátem meam ego cognósco: * et peccátum meum contra me est semper.

Tibi soli peccávi, et malum coram te feci: * ut iustificéris in sermónibus tuis, et vincas cum iudicáris.

Ecce enim, in iniquitátibus concéptus sum: * et in peccátis concépit me mater mea.

Ecce enim, veritátem dilexísti: * incérta et occúlta sapiéntiæ tuæ manifestásti mihi.

Aspérges me hyssópo, et mundábor: * lavábis me, et super nivem dealbábor.

As it was in the beginning, is now, * and ever shall be, world without end. Amen.

During the year, Ant. Have mercy upon me † O God.

And it is not repeated in the psalm.

Paschaltide, Ant. Alleluia, † alleluia, alleluia.

And the three following psalms are said under this one antiphon.

Psalm 50 [1]

Have mercy on me, O God, * according to thy great mercy.

And according to the multitude of thy tender mercies * blot out my iniquity.

Wash me yet more from my iniquity, * and cleanse me from my sin.

For I know my iniquity, * and my sin is always before me.

To thee only have I sinned, and have done evil before thee: * that thou mayst be justified in thy words, and mayst overcome when thou art judged.

For behold I was conceived in iniquities; * and in sins did my mother conceive me.

For behold thou hast loved truth: * the uncertain and hidden things of thy wisdom thou hast made manifest to me.

Thou shalt sprinkle me with hyssop, and I shall be cleansed: * thou shalt wash me, and I shall be made whiter than snow.

Monday - Lauds

Audítui meo dabis gáudium et lætítiam: * et exsultábunt ossa humiliáta.

Avérte fáciem tuam a peccátis meis: * et omnes iniquitátes meas dele.

Cor mundum crea in me, Deus: * et spíritum rectum ínnova in viscéribus meis.

Ne proícias me a fácie tua: * et spíritum sanctum tuum ne áuferas a me.

Redde mihi lætítiam salutáris tui: * et spíritu principáli confírma me.

Docébo iníquos vias tuas: * et ímpii ad te converténtur.

Líbera me de sanguínibus, Deus, Deus salútis meæ: * et exsultábit lingua mea iustítiam tuam.

Dómine, lábia mea apéries: * et os meum annuntiábit laudem tuam.

Quóniam si voluísses sacrifícium, dedíssem útique: * holocáustis non delectáberis.

Sacrifícium Deo spíritus contribulátus: * cor contrítum, et humiliátum, Deus, non despícies.

Benígne fac, Dómine, in bona voluntáte tua Sion: * ut ædificéntur muri Ierúsalem.

Tunc acceptábis sacrifícium iustítiæ, oblatiónes, et holocáusta:

To my hearing thou shalt give joy and gladness: * and the bones that have been humbled shall rejoice.

Turn away thy face from my sins, * and blot out all my iniquities.

Create a clean heart in me, O God: * and renew a right spirit within my bowels.

Cast me not away from thy face; * and take not thy holy spirit from me.

Restore unto me the joy of thy salvation, * and strengthen me with a perfect spirit.

I will teach the unjust thy ways: * and the wicked shall be converted to thee.

Deliver me from blood, O God, thou God of my salvation: * and my tongue shall extol thy justice.

O Lord, thou wilt open my lips: * and my mouth shall declare thy praise.

For if thou hadst desired sacrifice, I would indeed have given it: * with burnt offerings thou wilt not be delighted.

A sacrifice to God is an afflicted spirit: * a contrite and humbled heart, O God, thou wilt not despise.

Deal favourably, O Lord, in thy good will with Sion; * that the walls of Jerusalem may be built up.

Then shalt thou accept the sacrifice of justice, oblations and whole burnt offerings: * then

22   *Monday - Lauds*

* tunc impónent super altáre tuum vítulos.

Ant. Miserére mei, Deus.

Ant. Intéllege † clamórem meum, Dómine.

Psalmus 5 [2]

VERBA mea áuribus pércipe, Dómine, * intéllege clamórem meum.

Inténde voci oratiónis meæ, * Rex meus et Deus meus.

Quóniam ad te orábo: * Dómine, mane exáudies vocem meam.

Mane astábo tibi et vidébo: * quóniam non Deus volens iniquitátem tu es.

Neque habitábit iuxta te malígnus: * neque permanébunt iniústi ante óculos tuos.

Odísti omnes, qui operántur iniquitátem: * perdes omnes, qui loquúntur mendácium.

Virum sánguinum et dolósum abominábitur Dóminus: * ego autem in multitúdine misericórdiæ tuæ.

Introíbo in domum tuam: * adorábo ad templum sanctum tuum in timóre tuo.

Dómine, deduc me in iustítia tua: * propter inimícos meos dírige in conspéctu tuo viam meam.

Quóniam non est in ore eórum véritas: * cor eórum vanum est.

Sepúlcrum patens est guttur eórum, † linguis suis dolóse agébant, * iúdica illos, Deus.

---

shall they lay calves upon thy altar.

Ant. Have mercy upon me O God.

Ant. Hearken to my cry † O Lord.

Psalm 5 [2]

GIVE ear, O Lord, to my words * understand my cry.

Hearken to the voice of my prayer, * O my King and my God.

For to thee will I pray: * O Lord, in the morning thou shalt hear my voice.

In the morning I will stand before thee, and will see: * because thou art not a God that willest iniquity.

Neither shall the wicked dwell near thee: * nor shall the unjust abide before thy eyes.

Thou hatest all the workers of iniquity: * thou wilt destroy all that speak a lie.

The bloody and the deceitful man the Lord will abhor. * But as for me in the multitude of thy mercy,

I will come into thy house; * I will worship towards thy holy temple, in thy fear.

Conduct me, O Lord, in thy justice: * because of my enemies, direct my way in thy sight.

For there is no truth in their mouth: * their heart is vain.

Their throat is an open sepulchre: † they dealt deceitfully with their tongues: * judge them, O God.

Monday - Lauds

Décidant a cogitatiónibus suis, † secúndum multitúdinem impietátum eórum expélle eos, * quóniam irritavérunt te, Dómine.

Et læténtur omnes, qui sperant in te, * in ætérnum exsultábunt: et habitábis in eis.

Et gloriabúntur in te omnes, qui díligunt nomen tuum, * quóniam tu benedíces iusto.

Dómine, ut scuto bonæ voluntátis tuæ * coronásti nos.

Ant. Intéllege clamórem meum, Dómine.

Ant. Dómine, † in cælo misericórdia tua.

Psalmus 35 [3]

DIXIT iniústus ut delínquat in semetípso: * non est timor Dei ante óculos eius.

Quóniam dolóse egit in conspéctu eius: * ut inveniátur iníquitas eius ad ódium.

Verba oris eius iníquitas, et dolus: * nóluit intellégere ut bene ágeret.

Iniquitátem meditátus est in cubíli suo: † ástitit omni viæ non bonæ, * malítiam autem non odívit.

Dómine, in cælo misericórdia tua: * et véritas tua usque ad nubes.

Iustítia tua sicut montes Dei: * iudícia tua abýssus multa.

Let them fall from their devices: † according to the multitude of their wickednesses cast them out: * for they have provoked thee, O Lord.

But let all them be glad that hope in thee: * they shall rejoice for ever, and thou shalt dwell in them.

And all they that love thy name shall glory in thee: * For thou wilt bless the just.

O Lord, thou hast crowned us, * as with a shield of thy good will.

Ant. Hearken to my cry O Lord.

Ant. Thy mercy, † O Lord, is in the heavens

Psalm 35 [3]

THE unjust hath said within himself, that he would sin: * there is no fear of God before his eyes.

For in his sight he hath done deceitfully, * that his iniquity may be found unto hatred.

The words of his mouth are iniquity and guile: * he would not understand that he might do well.

He hath devised iniquity on his bed, † he hath set himself on every way that is not good: * but evil he hath not hated.

O Lord, thy mercy is in heaven, * and thy truth reacheth even to the clouds.

Thy justice is as the mountains of God, * thy judgments are a great deep.

Hómines, et iuménta salvábis, Dómine: * quemádmodum multiplicásti misericórdiam tuam, Deus.

Fílii autem hóminum, * in tégmine alárum tuárum sperábunt.

Inebriabúntur ab ubertáte domus tuæ: * et torrénte voluptátis tuæ potábis eos.

Quóniam apud te est fons vitæ: * et in lúmine tuo vidébimus lumen.

Præténde misericórdiam tuam sciéntibus te, * et iustítiam tuam his, qui recto sunt corde.

Non véniat mihi pes supérbiæ: * et manus peccatóris non móveat me.

Ibi cecidérunt qui operántur iniquitátem: * expúlsi sunt, nec potuérunt stare.

Ant. Dómine, in cælo misericórdia tua.

Tempore paschali, Ant. Allelúia, allelúia, allelúia.

Men and beasts thou wilt preserve, O Lord: * O how hast thou multiplied thy mercy, O God!

But the children of men * shall put their trust under the covert of thy wings.

They shall be inebriated with the plenty of thy house; * and thou shalt make them drink of the torrent of thy pleasure.

For with thee is the fountain of life; * and in thy light we shall see light.

Extend thy mercy to them that know thee, * and thy justice to them that are right in heart.

Let not the foot of pride come to me, * and let not the hand of the sinner move me.

There the workers of iniquity are fallen, * they are cast out, and could not stand.

Ant. Thy mercy, O Lord, is in the heavens

Paschaltide, ant. Alleluia, alleluia, alleluia.

Canticum Feriale

Ant. Convérsus est † furor tuus, Dómine, et consolátus es me. (*T.P.* Allelúia.)

Canticum Isaiæ [4]

Isa. 12:1-6

CONFITÉBOR tibi, Dómine, quóniam irátus es mihi: * convérsus est furor tuus, et consolátus es me.

Ferial Canticle

Ant. Thy wrath is turned away, † O Lord, and Thou hast comforted me. (*P.T.* Alleluia.)

Canticle of Isaias [4]

Is. 12:1-6

I thank Thee, O Lord though Thou wast angry with me, * Thy wrath is turned away and Thou has comforted me.

Ecce Deus salvátor meus, * fiducíaliter agam, et non timébo:

Quia fortitúdo mea et laus mea Dóminus, * et factus est mihi in salútem.

Hauriétis aquas in gáudio de fóntibus Salvatóris. † Et dicétis in die illa: * Confitémini Dómino, et invocáte nomen eius:

Notas fácite in pópulis adinventiónes eius: * mementóte, quóniam excélsum est nomen eius.

Cantáte Dómino, quóniam magnífice fecit: * annuniáte hoc in univérsa terra.

Exsúlta et lauda, habitátio Sion: * quia magnus in médio tui Sanctus Israël.

Ant. Convérsus est furor tuus, Dómine, et consolátus es me. (*T.P.* Allelúia.)

Canticum Festivum
Ant. Laudámus nomen tuum † ínclitum, Deus noster. (*T.P.* Allelúia.)

Canticum David [4]
1 Par. 29:10-13

Benedíctus es, Dómine, Deus Israël patris nostri, * ab ætérno in ætérnum.

Tua est, Dómine, magnificéntia, et poténtia, * et glória, atque victória:

Behold, God is my salvation, * I am full of confidence and not afraid;

For the Lord is my strength and my song of praise, * and He is become my salvation.

And with joy you shall draw water from the fountains of salvation. † And you shall say on that day: * Praise the Lord, call upon His Name!

Make His works known among the nations, * declare how exalted is His Name!

Sing praise to the Lord, for He hath done great things; * let this be known in all the earth!

Rejoice and shout for joy, O thou inhabitant of Sion, * for great in the midst of thee is the Holy One of Israel!

Ant. Thy wrath is turned away, O Lord, and Thou hast comforted me. (*P.T.* Alleluia.)

Festal Canticle
Ant. O God of majesty † we praise thy glorious name. (*P.T.* Alleluia.)

Canticle of David [4]
1 Chron. 29:10-13

Blessed art thou, O Lord the God of Israel, our father * from eternity to eternity.

Thine, O Lord, is magnificence, and power, * and glory, and victory:

Et tibi laus: * cuncta enim quæ in cælo sunt, et in terra, tua sunt:

Tuum, Dómine, regnum, * et tu es super omnes príncipes.
Tuæ divítiæ, et tua est glória: * tu domináris ómnium,

In manu tua virtus et poténtia: * in manu tua magnitúdo, et impérium ómnium.
Nunc ígitur, Deus noster, confitémur tibi, * et laudámus nomen tuum ínclitum.
Ant. Laudámus nomen tuum ínclitum, Deus noster. (*T.P.* Allelúia.)

Ant. Laudáte † Dóminum de cælis.
Tempore paschali, Ant. Allelúia, † allelúia, allelúia.

Psalmus 148 [5]

LAUDÁTE Dóminum de cælis: * laudáte eum in excélsis.

Laudáte eum, omnes Angeli eius: * laudáte eum, omnes virtútes eius.
Laudáte eum, sol et luna: * laudáte eum, omnes stellæ et lumen.
Laudáte eum, cæli cælórum: * et aquæ omnes, quæ super cælos sunt, laudent nomen Dómini.

Quia ipse dixit, et facta sunt: * ipse mandávit, et creáta sunt.

And to thee is praise: * for all that is in heaven, and in earth, is thine:
Thine is the kingdom, O Lord, * and thou art above all princes.
Thine are riches, and thine is glory, * thou hast dominion over all,
In thy hand is power and might: * in thy hand greatness, and the empire of all things.
Now therefore our God we give thanks to thee, * and we praise thy glorious name.
Ant. Thy wrath is turned away, O Lord, and Thou hast comforted me. (*P.T.* Alleluia.)

Ant. Praise ye † the Lord from the heavens.
Paschaltide, Ant. Alleluia, † alleluia, alleluia.

Psalm 148 [5]

PRAISE ye the Lord from the heavens * praise ye him in the high places.
Praise ye him, all his angels: * praise ye him, all his hosts.

Praise ye him, O sun and moon: * praise him, all ye stars and light.

Praise him, ye heavens of heavens: * and let all the waters that are above the heavens, praise the name of the Lord.
For he spoke, and they were made: * he commanded, and they were created.

Monday - Lauds

Státuit ea in ætérnum, et in sæculum sǽculi: * præcéptum pósuit, et non præteríbit.

Laudáte Dóminum de terra, * dracónes, et omnes abýssi.

Ignis, grando, nix, glácies, spíritus procellárum: * quæ fáciunt verbum eius:

Montes, et omnes colles: * ligna fructífera, et omnes cedri.

Béstiæ, et univérsa pécora: * serpéntes, et vólucres pennátæ:

Reges terræ, et omnes pópuli: * príncipes, et omnes iúdices terræ.

Iúvenes, et vírgines: † senes cum iunióribus laudent nomen Dómini: * quia exaltátum est nomen eius solíus.

Conféssio eius super cælum et terram: * et exaltávit cornu pópuli sui.

Hymnus ómnibus sanctis eius: * fíliis Israël, pópulo appropinquánti sibi.

Hic non dicitur Gloria Patri.

Psalmus 149 [6]

CANTÁTE Dómino cánticum novum: * laus eius in ecclésia sanctórum.

Lætétur Israël in eo, qui fecit eum: * et fílii Sion exsúltent in rege suo.

Laudent nomen eius in choro: * in týmpano, et psaltério psallant ei:

Quia beneplácitum est Dómino in pópulo suo: * et exaltábit mansuétos in salútem.

He hath established them for ever, and for ages of ages: * he hath made a decree, and it shall not pass away.

Praise the Lord from the earth, * ye dragons, and all ye deeps:

Fire, hail, snow, ice, stormy winds * which fulfill his word:

Mountains and all hills, * fruitful trees and all cedars:

Beasts and all cattle: * serpents and feathered fowls:

Kings of the earth and all people: * princes and all judges of the earth:

Young men and maidens: † let the old with the younger, praise the name of the Lord: * For his name alone is exalted.

The praise of him is above heaven and earth: * and he hath exalted the horn of his people.

A hymn to all his saints: to the children of Israel, a people approaching him.

Here the Glory be is not said.

Psalm 149 [6]

SING ye to the Lord a new canticle: * let his praise be in the church of the saints.

Let Israel rejoice in him that made him: * and let the children of Sion be joyful in their king.

Let them praise his name in choir: * let them sing to him with the timbrel and the psaltery.

For the Lord is well pleased with his people: * and he will exalt the meek unto salvation.

Monday - Lauds

Exsultábunt sancti in glória: * lætabúntur in cubílibus suis.

Exaltatiónes Dei in gútture eórum: * et gládii ancípites in mánibus eórum.

Ad faciéndam vindíctam in natiónibus: * increpatiónes in pópulis.

Ad alligándos reges eórum in compédibus: * et nóbiles eórum in mánicis férreis.

Ut fáciant in eis iudícium conscríptum: * glória hæc est ómnibus sanctis eius.

Hic non dicitur Gloria Patri.

Psalmus 150 [7]

LAUDÁTE Dóminum in sanctis eius: * laudáte eum in firmaménto virtútis eius.

Laudáte eum in virtútibus eius: * laudáte eum secúndum multitúdinem magnitúdinis eius.

Laudáte eum in sono tubæ: * laudáte eum in psaltério, et cíthara.

Laudáte eum in týmpano, et choro: * laudáte eum in chordis, et órgano.

Laudáte eum in cýmbalis benesonántibus: † laudáte eum in cýmbalis iubilatiónis: * omnis spíritus laudet Dóminum.

Glória Patri, et Fílio, * et Spirítui Sancto.

Sicut erat in princípio, et nunc, et semper, * et in sǽcula sæculórum. Amen.

Ant. Laudáte Dóminum de cælis.

The saints shall rejoice in glory: * they shall be joyful in their beds.

The high praises of God shall be in their mouth: * and two-edged swords in their hands:

To execute vengeance upon the nations, * chastisements among the people:

To bind their kings with fetters, * and their nobles with manacles of iron.

To execute upon them the judgment that is written: * this glory is to all his saints.

Here the Glory be is not said.

Psalm 150 [7]

PRAISE ye the Lord in his holy places: * praise ye him in the firmament of his power.

Praise ye him for his mighty acts: * praise ye him according to the multitude of his greatness.

Praise him with sound of trumpet: * praise him with psaltery and harp.

Praise him with timbrel and choir: * praise him with strings and organs.

Praise him on high sounding cymbals: † praise him on cymbals of joy: * let every spirit praise the Lord.

Glory be to the Father, and to the Son, * and to the Holy Ghost.

As it was in the beginning, is now, * and ever shall be, world without end. Amen.

Ant. Praise ye the Lord from the heavens.

Monday - Lauds

Tempore paschali, Ant. Allelúia, allelúia, allelúia.

Capitulum *Rom. 13:12-13*

Nox præcéssit, dies autem appropinquávit. † Abiciámus ergo ópera tenebrárum, et induámur arma lucis. * Sicut in die honéste ambulémus. ℟. Deo grátias.

℟.*br.* Sana ánimam meam, * quia peccávi tibi.
℟. Sana ánimam meam, * quia peccávi tibi.
℣. Ego dixi: Dómine, miserére mei
℟. Quia peccávi tibi.

℣. Glória Patri, et Fílio, * et Spirítui Sancto.

℟. Sana ánimam meam, * quia peccávi tibi.

Hymnus
Splendor patérnæ glóriæ,
De luce lucem próferens,
Lux lucis, et fons lúminis,
Diem dies illúminans:

Verúsque sol illábere,
Micans nitóre pérpeti:
Iubárque Sancti Spíritus
Infúnde nostris sénsibus.

Votis vocémus et Patrem,
Patrem perénnis glóriæ,
Patrem poténtis grátiæ,
Culpam reléget lúbricam.

Paschaltide, Ant. Alleluia, alleluia, alleluia.

Chapter *Rom. 13:12-13*

The night is passed, and the day is at hand. Let us therefore cast off the works of darkness, and put on the armour of light. Let us walk honestly, as in the day. ℟. Thanks be to God.

℟.*br.* Heal my soul, * for I have sinned against thee.
℟. Heal my soul, * for I have sinned against thee.
℣. I said: O Lord, be thou merciful to me
℟. For I have sinned against thee.

℣. Glory be to the Father, and to the Son, * and to the Holy Ghost.

℟. Heal my soul, * for I have sinned against thee.

Hymn
O splendour of God's glory bright,
O thou that bringest light from light,
O light of light, light's living spring,
O day, all days illumining.

O thou true sun, on us thy glance
Let fall in royal radiance,
The Spirit's sanctifying beam
Upon our earthly senses stream.

The Father too our prayers implore,
Father of glory evermore,
The Father of all grace and might,
To banish sin from our delight:

Monday - Lauds

Confírmet actus strénuos:
Dentes retúndat ínvidi:
Casus secúndet ásperos,
Donet geréndi grátiam.

Mentem gubérnet et regat,
Casto, fidéli córpore:
Fides calóre férveat,
Fraudis venéna nésciat.

Christúsque nobis sit cibus,
Potúsque noster sit fides:
Læti bibámus sóbriam
Ebrietátem spíritus.

Lætus dies hic tránseat,
Pudor sit ut dilúculum,
Fides velut merídies,
Crepúsculum mens nésciat.

Auróra cursus próvehit,
Auróra totus pródeat,
In Patre totus Fílius,
Et totus in Verbo Pater.

Deo Patri sit glória,
Eiúsque soli Fílio,
Cum Spíritu Paráclito,
Et nunc et in perpétuum.
Amen.

℣. Repléti sumus mane misericórdia tua.
℟. Exsultávimus, et delectáti sumus.

Ant. Benedíctus † Dóminus Deus Israël.
Et non repetitur in cantico.

To guide whate'er we nobly do,
With love all envy to subdue,
To make ill-fortune turn to fair,
And give us grace our wrongs to bear.

Our mind be in his keeping placed,
Our body true to him and chaste,
Where only faith her fire shall feed,
And burn the tares of Satan's seed.

And Christ to us for food shall be,
From him our drink that welleth free,
The Spirit's wine, that maketh whole,
And mocking not, exalts the soul.

Rejoicing may this day go hence,
Like virgin dawn our innocence,
Like fiery noon our faith appear,
Nor know the gloom of twilight drear.

Morn in her rosy car is borne;
Let him come forth our perfect morn,
The Word in God the Father One,
The Father perfect in the Son.

All laud to God the Father be;
All praise, Eternal Son, to thee;
All glory, as is ever meet,
To God the Holy Paraclete.
Amen.

℣. We are filled in the morning with thy mercy.
℟. And we have rejoiced, and are delighted.

Ant. Blessed be the Lord † the God of Israel.
It is not repeated in the canticle.

Canticum Zachariæ

Luc. 1:68-79

BENEDÍCTUS ✠ Dóminus, Deus Israël: * quia visitávit, et fecit redemptiónem plebis suæ:

Et eréxit cornu salútis nobis: * in domo David, púeri sui.

Sicut locútus est per os sanctórum, * qui a sǽculo sunt, prophetárum eius:

Salútem ex inimícis nostris, * et de manu ómnium, qui odérunt nos.

Ad faciéndam misericórdiam cum pátribus nostris: * et memorári testaménti sui sancti.

Iusiurándum, quod iurávit ad Abraham patrem nostrum, * datúrum se nobis:

Ut sine timóre, de manu inimicórum nostrórum liberáti, * serviámus illi.

In sanctitáte, et iustítia coram ipso, * ómnibus diébus nostris.

Et tu, puer, Prophéta Altíssimi vocáberis: * præíbis enim ante fáciem Dómini, paráre vias eius:

Ad dandam sciéntiam salútis plebi eius: * in remissiónem peccatórum eórum:

Per víscera misericórdiæ Dei nostri: * in quibus visitávit nos, óriens ex alto:

Illumináre his, qui in ténebris, et in umbra mortis sedent: * ad dirigéndos pedes nostros in viam pacis.

Canticle of Zacharias

Luke 1:68-79

Blessed be the Lord ✠ God of Israel; * because he hath visited and wrought the redemption of his people:

And hath raised up an horn of salvation to us, * in the house of David his servant:

As he spoke by the mouth of his holy Prophets, * who are from the beginning:

Salvation from our enemies, * and from the hand of all that hate us:

To perform mercy to our fathers, * and to remember his holy testament,

The oath, which he swore to Abraham our father, * that he would grant to us,

That being delivered from the hand of our enemies, * we may serve him without fear,

In holiness and justice before him, * all our days.

And thou, child, shalt be called the prophet of the Highest: * for thou shalt go before the face of the Lord to prepare his ways:

To give knowledge of salvation to his people, * unto the remission of their sins:

Through the bowels of the mercy of our God, * in which the Orient from on high hath visited us:

To enlighten them that sit in darkness, and in the shadow of death: * to direct our feet into the way of peace.

Monday - Lauds

Ant. Benedíctus Dóminus Deus Israël.

Kýrie, eléison. Christe, eléison. Kýrie, eléison.

Pater noster, qui es in cælis, sanctificétur nomen tuum: advéniat regnum tuum: fiat volúntas tua, sicut in cælo et in terra. Panem nostrum cotidiánum da nobis hódie: et dimítte nobis débita nostra, sicut et nos dimíttimus debitóribus nostris:

℣. Et ne nos indúcas in tentatiónem:

℟. Sed líbera nos a malo.

℣. Dóminus vobíscum.

℟. Et cum spíritu tuo.

℣. Benedicámus Dómino.

℟. Deo grátias.

℣. Fidélium ánimæ per misericórdiam Dei requiéscant in pace.

℟. Amen.

℣. Divínum auxílium máneat semper nobíscum.

℟. Et cum frátribus nostris abséntibus. Amen.

Ant. Blessed be the Lord the God of Israel.

Lord have mercy upon us, Christ have mercy upon us, Lord have mercy upon us

Our Father, who art in heaven, Hallowed be thy name. Thy kingdom come. Thy will be done on earth as it is in heaven. Give us this day our daily bread. And forgive us our trespasses, as we forgive those who trespass against us.

℣. And lead us not into temptation:

℟. But deliver us from evil.

℣. The Lord be with you.

℟. And with your spirit.

℣. Let us bless the Lord.

℟. Thanks be to God.

℣. May the souls of the faithful, through the mercy of God, rest in peace.

℟. Amen.

℣. May the divine assistance remain with us always.

℟. And with our brothers, who are absent. Amen.

TUESDAY - LAUDS

℣. Deus in adiutórium meum inténde.

℟. Dómine, ad adiuvándum me festína. Glória Patri, et Fílio, * et Spirítui Sancto. Sicut erat in princípio, et nunc, et semper, * et in sǽcula sæculórum. Amen. Allelúia.

Psalmus 66

Deus misereátur nostri, et benedícat nobis: * illúminet vultum suum super nos, et misereátur nostri.

Ut cognoscámus in terra viam tuam, * in ómnibus géntibus salutáre tuum.

Confiteántur tibi pópuli, Deus: * confiteántur tibi pópuli omnes.

Læténtur et exsúltent gentes: † quóniam iúdicas pópulos in æquitáte, * et gentes in terra dírigis.

Confiteántur tibi pópuli, Deus, † confiteántur tibi pópuli omnes: * terra dedit fructum suum.

Benedícat nos Deus, Deus noster, benedícat nos Deus: * et métuant eum omnes fines terræ.

Glória Patri, et Fílio, * et Spirítui Sancto.

℣. O God, come to my assistance;

℟. O Lord, make haste to help me. Glory be to the Father, and to the Son, * and to the Holy Ghost. As it was in the beginning, is now, * and ever shall be, world without end. Amen. Alleluia.

Psalm 66

May God have mercy on us, and bless us: * may he cause the light of his countenance to shine upon us, and may he have mercy on us.

That we may know thy way upon earth: * thy salvation in all nations.

Let people confess to thee, O God: * let all people give praise to thee.

Let the nations be glad and rejoice: † for thou judgest the people with justice, * and directest the nations upon earth.

Let the people, O God, confess to thee: † let all the people give praise to thee: * the earth hath yielded her fruit.

May God, our God bless us, may God bless us: * and all the ends of the earth fear him.

Glory be to the Father, and to the Son, * and to the Holy Ghost.

Tuesday - Lauds

Sicut erat in princípio, et nunc, et semper, * et in sǽcula sæculórum. Amen.

Per annum, Ant. Dele, Dómine, † iniquitátem meam.

Tempore paschali, Ant. Allelúia, † allelúia, allelúia.

Et dicitur tres psalmi sequentes sub una antiphona.

Psalmus 50 [1]

Miserére mei, Deus, * secúndum magnam misericórdiam tuam.

Et secúndum multitúdinem miseratiónum tuárum, * dele iniquitátem meam.

Amplius lava me ab iniquitáte mea: * et a peccáto meo munda me.

Quóniam iniquitátem meam ego cognósco: * et peccátum meum contra me est semper.

Tibi soli peccávi, et malum coram te feci: * ut iustificéris in sermónibus tuis, et vincas cum iudicáris.

Ecce enim, in iniquitátibus concéptus sum: * et in peccátis concépit me mater mea.

Ecce enim, veritátem dilexísti: * incérta et occúlta sapiéntiæ tuæ manifestásti mihi.

Aspérges me hyssópo, et mundábor: * lavábis me, et super nivem dealbábor.

Audítui meo dabis gáudium et lætítiam: * et exsultábunt ossa humiliáta.

As it was in the beginning, is now, * and ever shall be, world without end. Amen.

During the year, Ant. Blot out, O Lord † my iniquity.

Paschaltide, Ant. Alleluia, † alleluia, alleluia.

And the three following psalms are said under this one antiphon.

Psalm 50 [1]

Have mercy on me, O God, * according to thy great mercy.

And according to the multitude of thy tender mercies * blot out my iniquity.

Wash me yet more from my iniquity, * and cleanse me from my sin.

For I know my iniquity, * and my sin is always before me.

To thee only have I sinned, and have done evil before thee: * that thou mayst be justified in thy words, and mayst overcome when thou art judged.

For behold I was conceived in iniquities; * and in sins did my mother conceive me.

For behold thou hast loved truth: * the uncertain and hidden things of thy wisdom thou hast made manifest to me.

Thou shalt sprinkle me with hyssop, and I shall be cleansed: * thou shalt wash me, and I shall be made whiter than snow.

To my hearing thou shalt give joy and gladness: * and the bones that have been humbled shall rejoice.

Tuesday - Lauds

Avérte fáciem tuam a peccátis meis: * et omnes iniquitátes meas dele.

Cor mundum crea in me, Deus: * et spíritum rectum ínnova in viscéribus meis.

Ne proícias me a fácie tua: * et spíritum sanctum tuum ne áuferas a me.

Redde mihi lætítiam salutáris tui: * et spíritu principáli confírma me.

Docébo iníquos vias tuas: * et ímpii ad te converténtur.

Líbera me de sanguínibus, Deus, Deus salútis meæ: * et exsultábit lingua mea iustítiam tuam.

Dómine, lábia mea apéries: * et os meum annuntiábit laudem tuam.

Quóniam si voluísses sacrifícium, dedíssem útique: * holocáustis non delectáberis.

Sacrifícium Deo spíritus contribulátus: * cor contrítum, et humiliátum, Deus, non despícies.

Benígne fac, Dómine, in bona voluntáte tua Sion: * ut ædificéntur muri Ierúsalem.

Tunc acceptábis sacrifícium iustítiæ, oblatiónes, et holocáusta: * tunc impónent super altáre tuum vítulos.

Ant. Dele, Dómine, iniquitátem meam.

Turn away thy face from my sins, * and blot out all my iniquities.

Create a clean heart in me, O God: * and renew a right spirit within my bowels.

Cast me not away from thy face; * and take not thy holy spirit from me.

Restore unto me the joy of thy salvation, * and strengthen me with a perfect spirit.

I will teach the unjust thy ways: * and the wicked shall be converted to thee.

Deliver me from blood, O God, thou God of my salvation: * and my tongue shall extol thy justice.

O Lord, thou wilt open my lips: * and my mouth shall declare thy praise.

For if thou hadst desired sacrifice, I would indeed have given it: * with burnt offerings thou wilt not be delighted.

A sacrifice to God is an afflicted spirit: * a contrite and humbled heart, O God, thou wilt not despise.

Deal favourably, O Lord, in thy good will with Sion; * that the walls of Jerusalem may be built up.

Then shalt thou accept the sacrifice of justice, oblations and whole burnt offerings: * then shall they lay calves upon thy altar.

Ant. Blot out, O Lord my iniquity.

36   *Tuesday - Lauds*

Ant. Salutáre † vultus mei, et Deus meus.

Psalmus 42 [2]

Iúdica me, Deus, et discérne causam meam de gente non sancta, * ab hómine iníquo, et dolóso érue me.

Quia tu es, Deus, fortitúdo mea: † quare me repulísti? * et quare tristis incédo, dum afflígit me inimícus?

Emítte lucem tuam et veritátem tuam: † ipsa me deduxérunt, et adduxérunt in montem sanctum tuum, * et in tabernácula tua.

Et introíbo ad altáre Dei: * ad Deum, qui lætíficat iuventútem meam.

Confitébor tibi in cíthara, Deus, Deus meus: * quare tristis es, ánima mea? et quare contúrbas me?

Spera in Deo, quóniam adhuc confitébor illi: * salutáre vultus mei, et Deus meus.

Ant. Salutáre vultus mei, et Deus meus.

Ant. Quóniam † in te confídit ánima mea.

Psalmus 56 [3]

Miserére mei, Deus, miserére mei: * quóniam in te confídit ánima mea.

Et in umbra alárum tuárum sperábo, * donec tránseat iníquitas.

Clamábo ad Deum altíssimum: * Deum qui benefécit mihi.

Ant. The salvation † of my countenance and my God.

Psalm 42 [2]

Judge me, O God, and distinguish my cause from the nation that is not holy: * deliver me from the unjust and deceitful man.

For thou art God my strength: † why hast thou cast me off? * and why do I go sorrowful whilst the enemy afflicteth me?

Send forth thy light and thy truth: † they have conducted me, and brought me unto thy holy hill, * and into thy tabernacles.

And I will go in to the altar of God: * to God who giveth joy to my youth.

To thee, O God my God, I will give praise upon the harp: * why art thou sad, O my soul? and why dost thou disquiet me?

Hope in God, for I will still give praise to him: * the salvation of my countenance, and my God

Ant. The salvation of my countenance and my God.

Ant. For in thee † my soul trusteth.

Psalm 56 [3]

Have mercy on me, O God, have mercy on me: * for my soul trusteth in thee.

And in the shadow of thy wings will I hope, * until iniquity pass away.

I will cry to God the most High; * to God who hath done good to me.

Tuesday - Lauds 37

Misit de cælo, et liberávit me: * dedit in oppróbrium conculcántes me.

Misit Deus misericórdiam suam, et veritátem suam, † et erípuit ánimam meam de médio catulórum leónum: * dormívi conturbátus.

Fílii hóminum dentes eórum arma et sagíttæ: * et lingua eórum gládius acútus.

Exaltáre super cælos, Deus, * et in omnem terram glória tua.

Láqueum paravérunt pédibus meis: * et incurvavérunt ánimam meam.

Fodérunt ante fáciem meam fóveam: * et incidérunt in eam.

Parátum cor meum, Deus, parátum cor meum: * cantábo, et psalmum dicam.

Exsúrge, glória mea, exsúrge, psaltérium et cíthara: * exsúrgam dilúculo.

Confitébor tibi in pópulis, Dómine: * et psalmum dicam tibi in géntibus:

Quóniam magnificáta est usque ad cælos misericórdia tua, * et usque ad nubes véritas tua.

Exaltáre super cælos, Deus: * et super omnem terram glória tua.

Per annum, Ant. Quóniam in te confídit ánima mea.

Tempore paschali, Ant. Allelúia, allelúia, allelúia.

He hath sent from heaven and delivered me: * he hath made them a reproach that trod upon me.

God hath sent his mercy and his truth, † and he hath delivered my soul from the midst of the young lions. * I slept troubled.

The sons of men, whose teeth are weapons and arrows, * and their tongue a sharp sword.

Be thou exalted, O God, above the heavens, * and thy glory above all the earth.

They prepared a snare for my feet; * and they bowed down my soul.

They dug a pit before my face, * and they are fallen into it.

My heart is ready, O God, my heart is ready: * I will sing, and rehearse a psalm.

Arise, O my glory, arise psaltery and harp: * I will arise early.

I will give praise to thee, O Lord, among the people: * I will sing a psalm to thee among the nations.

For thy mercy is magnified even to the heavens: * and thy truth unto the clouds.

Be thou exalted, O God, above the heavens: * and thy glory above all the earth.

During the year, Ant. For in thee my soul trusteth.

Paschaltide, Ant. Alleluia, alleluia, alleluia.

Canticum Feriale

Ant. Cunctis diébus † vitæ nostræ salvos nos fac Dómine. (*T.P.* Allelúia.)

Canticum Ezechiæ [4]

Isa. 38:10-12

EGO dixi in dimídio diérum meórum: * Vadam ad portas ínferi.

Quæsívi resíduum annórum meórum. * Dixi: Non vidébo Dóminum Deum in terra vivéntium.

Non aspíciam hóminem ultra, * et habitatórem quiétis.

Generátio mea abláta est, et convolúta est a me, * quasi tabernáculum pastórum.

Præcísa est velut a texénte vita mea; † dum adhuc ordírer, succídit me: * de mane usque ad vésperam fínies me.

Sperábam usque ad mane; * quasi leo, sic contrívit ómnia ossa mea:

De mane usque ad vésperam fínies me. † Sicut pullus hirúndinis, sic clamábo; * meditábor ut colúmba.

Attenuáti sunt óculi mei, * suspiciéntes in excélsum.

Dómine, vim pátior, respónde pro me. * Quid dicam, aut quid respondébit mihi, cum ipse fécerit?

Recogitábo tibi omnes annos meos * in amaritúdine ánimæ meæ.

Ferial Canticle

Ant. All the days † of our life, make us safe, O Lord. (*P.T.* Alleluia.)

Canticle of Ezechias [4]

Is. 38:10-12

I said: In the midst of my days * I shall go to the gates of hell:

I sought for the remainder of my years. * I said: I shall not see the Lord God in the land of the living.

I shall behold man no more, nor the inhabitant of rest.

My generation is at an end, and it is rolled away from me, * as a shepherd's tent.

My life is cut off, as by a weaver: † whilst I was yet but beginning, he cut me off: * from morning even to night thou wilt make an end of me.

I hoped till morning, * as a lion so hath he broken all my bones:

From morning even to night thou wilt make an end of me. * I will cry like a young swallow, I will meditate like a dove:

My eyes are weakened * looking upward:

Lord, I suffer violence, answer thou for me. * What shall I say, or what shall he answer for me, whereas he himself hath done it?

I will recount to thee all my years * in the bitterness of my soul.

Tuesday - Lauds

Dómine, si sic vívitur, et in tálibus vita spíritus mei, † corrípies me, et vivificábis me. * Ecce in pace amaritúdo mea amaríssima.

Tu autem eruísti ánimam meam ut non períret; * proiecísti post tergum tuum ómnia peccáta mea.

Quia non inférnus confitébitur tibi, † neque mors laudábit te: * non exspectábunt qui descéndunt in lacum veritátem tuam.

Vivens, vivens ipse confitébitur tibi, sicut et ego hódie; * pater fíliis notam fáciet veritátem tuam.

Dómine, salvum me fac, * et psalmos nostros cantábimus cunctis diébus vitæ nostræ in domo Dómini.

Ant. Cunctis diébus vitæ nostræ salvos nos fac Dómine. (*T.P.* Allelúia.)

Canticum Festivum

Ant. Exaltáte † Regem sæculórum in opéribus vestris. (*T.P.* Allelúia.)

Canticum Tobiæ [4]
Tob. 13:1-11

MAGNUS es, Dómine, in ætérnum, * et in ómnia sǽcula regnum tuum:

Quóniam tu flagéllas, et salvas: † dedúcis ad ínferos, et redúcis: * et non est qui effúgiat manum tuam.

O Lord, if man's life be such, and the life of my spirit be in such things as these, † thou shalt correct me, and make me to live. * Behold in peace is my bitterness most bitter:

But thou hast delivered my soul that it should not perish, * thou hast cast all my sins behind thy back.

For hell shall not confess to thee, † neither shall death praise thee: * nor shall they that go down into the pit, look for thy truth.

The living, the living, he shall give praise to thee, as I do this day: * the father shall make thy truth known to the children.

O Lord, save me, * and we will sing our psalms all the days of our life in the house of the Lord.

Ant. All the days of our life, make us safe, O Lord. (*P.T.* Alleluia.)

Festal Canticle

Ant. Extol † the King of ages in your works. (*P.T.* Alleluia.)

Canticle of Tobias [4]
Tob. 13:1-11

THOU art great, O Lord, for ever, * and thy kingdom is unto all ages:

For thou scourgest, and thou savest: † thou leadest down to hell, and bringest up again: * and

Confitémini Dómino, fílii Israël, * et in conspéctu géntium laudáte eum:

Quóniam ídeo dispérsit vos inter gentes, quæ ignórant eum, * ut vos enarrétis mirabília eius,

Et faciátis scire eos, * quia non est álius Deus omnípotens præter eum.

Ipse castigávit nos propter iniquitátes nostras: * et ipse salvábit nos propter misericórdiam suam.

Aspícite ergo quæ fecit nobíscum, † et cum timóre et tremóre confitémini illi: * Regémque sæculórum exaltáte in opéribus vestris.

Ego autem in terra captivitátis meæ confitébor illi: * quóniam osténdit maiestátem suam in gentem peccatrícem.

Convertímini ítaque, peccatóres, † et fácite iustítiam coram Deo, * credéntes quod fáciat vobíscum misericórdiam suam:

Ego autem, et ánima mea * in eo lætábimur.

Benedícite Dóminum, omnes elécti eius: * ágite dies lætítiæ, et confitémini illi.

Ant. Exaltáte Regem sæculórum in opéribus vestris. (*T.P.* Allelúia.)

___

Ant. Omnes Angeli eius, † laudáte Dóminum de cælis.

Tempore paschali, Ant. Allelúia, † allelúia, allelúia.

there is none that can escape thy hand.

Give glory to the Lord, ye children of Israel, * and praise him in the sight of the Gentiles:

Because he hath therefore scattered you among the Gentiles, who know not him, * that you may declare his wonderful works,

And make them know * that there is no other almighty God besides him.

He hath chastised us for our iniquities: * and he will save us for his own mercy.

See then what he hath done with us, † and with fear and trembling give ye glory to him: * and extol the eternal King of worlds in your works.

As for me, I will praise him in the land of my captivity: * because he hath shewn his majesty toward a sinful nation.

Be converted therefore, ye sinners, † and do justice before God, * believing that he will shew his mercy to you.

And I and my soul * will rejoice in him.

Bless ye the Lord, all his elect, * keep days of joy, and give glory to him.

Ant. Extol the King of ages in your works. (*P.T.* Alleluia.)

___

Ant. All ye His angels † Praise the Lord from the heavens.

Paschaltide, Ant. Alleluia, † alleluia, alleluia.

Psalmus 148 [5]

LAUDÁTE Dóminum de cælis: * laudáte eum in excélsis.

Laudáte eum, omnes Angeli eius: * laudáte eum, omnes virtútes eius.

Laudáte eum, sol et luna: * laudáte eum, omnes stellæ et lumen.

Laudáte eum, cæli cælórum: * et aquæ omnes, quæ super cælos sunt, laudent nomen Dómini.

Quia ipse dixit, et facta sunt: * ipse mandávit, et creáta sunt.

Státuit ea in ætérnum, et in sæculum sæculi: * præcéptum pósuit, et non præteríbit.

Laudáte Dóminum de terra, * dracónes, et omnes abýssi.

Ignis, grando, nix, glácies, spíritus procellárum: * quæ fáciunt verbum eius:

Montes, et omnes colles: * ligna fructífera, et omnes cedri.

Béstiæ, et univérsa pécora: * serpéntes, et vólucres pennátæ:

Reges terræ, et omnes pópuli: * príncipes, et omnes iúdices terræ.

Iúvenes, et vírgines: † senes cum iunióribus laudent nomen Dómini: * quia exaltátum est nomen eius solíus.

Conféssio eius super cælum et terram: * et exaltávit cornu pópuli sui.

Psalm 148 [5]

PRAISE ye the Lord from the heavens * praise ye him in the high places.

Praise ye him, all his angels: * praise ye him, all his hosts.

Praise ye him, O sun and moon: * praise him, all ye stars and light.

Praise him, ye heavens of heavens: * and let all the waters that are above the heavens, praise the name of the Lord.

For he spoke, and they were made: * he commanded, and they were created.

He hath established them for ever, and for ages of ages: * he hath made a decree, and it shall not pass away.

Praise the Lord from the earth, * ye dragons, and all ye deeps:

Fire, hail, snow, ice, stormy winds * which fulfill his word:

Mountains and all hills, * fruitful trees and all cedars:

Beasts and all cattle: * serpents and feathered fowls:

Kings of the earth and all people: * princes and all judges of the earth:

Young men and maidens: † let the old with the younger, praise the name of the Lord: * For his name alone is exalted.

The praise of him is above heaven and earth: * and he hath exalted the horn of his people.

Hymnus ómnibus sanctis eius: * fíliis Israël, pópulo appropinquánti sibi.

Hic non dicitur Gloria Patri.

Psalmus 149 [6]

CANTÁTE Dómino cánticum novum: * laus eius in ecclésia sanctórum.

Lætétur Israël in eo, qui fecit eum: * et fílii Sion exsúltent in rege suo.

Laudent nomen eius in choro: * in týmpano, et psaltério psallant ei:

Quia beneplácitum est Dómino in pópulo suo: * et exaltábit mansuétos in salútem.

Exsultábunt sancti in glória: * lætabúntur in cubílibus suis.

Exaltatiónes Dei in gútture eórum: * et gládii ancípites in mánibus eórum.

Ad faciéndam vindíctam in natiónibus: * increpatiónes in pópulis.

Ad alligándos reges eórum in compédibus: * et nóbiles eórum in mánicis férreis.

Ut fáciant in eis iudícium conscríptum: * glória hæc est ómnibus sanctis eius.

Hic non dicitur Gloria Patri.

Psalmus 150 [7]

LAUDÁTE Dóminum in sanctis eius: * laudáte eum in firmaménto virtútis eius.

A hymn to all his saints: to the children of Israel, a people approaching him.

Here the Glory be is not said.

Psalm 149 [6]

SING ye to the Lord a new canticle: * let his praise be in the church of the saints.

Let Israel rejoice in him that made him: * and let the children of Sion be joyful in their king.

Let them praise his name in choir: * let them sing to him with the timbrel and the psaltery.

For the Lord is well pleased with his people: * and he will exalt the meek unto salvation.

The saints shall rejoice in glory: * they shall be joyful in their beds.

The high praises of God shall be in their mouth: * and two-edged swords in their hands:

To execute vengeance upon the nations, * chastisements among the people:

To bind their kings with fetters, * and their nobles with manacles of iron.

To execute upon them the judgment that is written: * this glory is to all his saints.

Here the Glory be is not said.

Psalm 150 [7]

PRAISE ye the Lord in his holy places: * praise ye him in the firmament of his power.

Tuesday - Lauds

Laudáte eum in virtútibus eius: * laudáte eum secúndum multitúdinem magnitúdinis eius.

Laudáte eum in sono tubæ: * laudáte eum in psaltério, et cíthara.

Laudáte eum in týmpano, et choro: * laudáte eum in chordis, et órgano.

Laudáte eum in cýmbalis benesonántibus: † laudáte eum in cýmbalis iubilatiónis: * omnis spíritus laudet Dóminum.

Glória Patri, et Fílio, * et Spirítui Sancto.

Sicut erat in princípio, et nunc, et semper, * et in sǽcula sæculórum. Amen.

Ant. Omnes Angeli eius, laudáte Dóminum de cælis.

Tempore paschali, Ant. Allelúia, allelúia, allelúia.

Capitulum   *Rom. 13:12-13*

Nox præcéssit, dies autem appropinquávit. † Abiciámus ergo ópera tenebrárum, et induámur arma lucis. * Sicut in die honéste ambulémus.

℞. Deo grátias.

℞.*br.* Sana ánimam meam, * quia peccávi tibi.

℞. Sana ánimam meam, * quia peccávi tibi.

℣. Ego dixi: Dómine, miserére mei

℞. Quia peccávi tibi.

Praise ye him for his mighty acts: * praise ye him according to the multitude of his greatness.

Praise him with sound of trumpet: * praise him with psaltery and harp.

Praise him with timbrel and choir: * praise him with strings and organs.

Praise him on high sounding cymbals: † praise him on cymbals of joy: * let every spirit praise the Lord.

Glory be to the Father, and to the Son, * and to the Holy Ghost.

As it was in the beginning, is now, * and ever shall be, world without end. Amen.

Ant. All ye His angels, praise the Lord from the heavens.

Paschaltide, Ant. Alleluia, alleluia, alleluia.

Chapter   *Rom. 13:12-13*

The night is passed, and the day is at hand. Let us therefore cast off the works of darkness, and put on the armour of light. Let us walk honestly, as in the day.

℞. Thanks be to God.

℞.*br.* Heal my soul, * for I have sinned against thee.

℞. Heal my soul, * for I have sinned against thee.

℣. I said: O Lord, be thou merciful to me

℞. For I have sinned against thee.

℣. Glória Patri, et Fílio, * et Spirítui Sancto.

℟. Sana ánimam meam, * quia peccávi tibi.

Hymnus

Ales diéi núntius
Lucem propínquam præcinit:
Nos excitátor méntium
Iam Christus ad vitam vocat.

Auférte, clamat, léctulos,
Ægro sopóre désides:
Castíque, recti, ac sóbrii
Vigiláte, iam sum próximus.

Iesum ciámus vócibus,
Flentes, precántes, sóbrii:
Inténta supplicátio
Dormíre cor mundum vetat.

Tu, Christe, somnum díscute:
Tu rumpe noctis víncula:
Tu solve peccátum vetus,
Novúmque lumen íngere.

Deo Patri sit glória,
Eiúsque soli Fílio,
Cum Spíritu Paráclito,
Et nunc et in perpétuum.
Amen.

℣. Repléti sumus mane misericórdia tua.
℟. Exsultávimus, et delectáti sumus.

Ant. Eréxit nobis † Dóminus cornu salútis in domo David púeri sui.

℣. Glory be to the Father, and to the Son, * and to the Holy Ghost.

℟. Heal my soul, * for I have sinned against thee.

Hymn

As the bird, whose clarion gay
Sounds before the dawn is grey,
Christ, who brings the spirit's day,
Calls us, close at hand:

Wake! he cries, and for my sake,
From your eyes dull slumbers shake!
Sober, righteous, chaste, awake!
At the door I stand!

Lord, to thee we lift on high
Fervent prayer and bitter cry:
Hearts aroused to pray and sigh
May not slumber more:

Break the sleep of death and time,
Forged by Adam's ancient crime;
And the light of Eden's prime
To the world restore!

All laud to God the Father be;
All praise, Eternal Son, to thee;
All glory, as is ever meet,
To God the Holy Paraclete.
Amen.

℣. We are filled in the morning with thy mercy.
℟. And we have rejoiced, and are delighted.

Ant. The Lord has raised up † a horn of salvation for us in the house of David his servant.

Canticum Zachariæ

Luc. 1:68-79

BENEDÍCTUS ✠ Dóminus, Deus Israël: * quia visitávit, et fecit redemptiónem plebis suæ:

Et eréxit cornu salútis nobis: * in domo David, púeri sui.

Sicut locútus est per os sanctórum, * qui a sǽculo sunt, prophetárum eius:

Salútem ex inimícis nostris, * et de manu ómnium, qui odérunt nos.

Ad faciéndam misericórdiam cum pátribus nostris: * et memorári testaménti sui sancti.

Iusiurándum, quod iurávit ad Abraham patrem nostrum, * datúrum se nobis:

Ut sine timóre, de manu inimicórum nostrórum liberáti, * serviámus illi.

In sanctitáte, et iustítia coram ipso, * ómnibus diébus nostris.

Et tu, puer, Prophéta Altíssimi vocáberis: * præíbis enim ante fáciem Dómini, paráre vias eius:

Ad dandam sciéntiam salútis plebi eius: * in remissiónem peccatórum eórum:

Per víscera misericórdiæ Dei nostri: * in quibus visitávit nos, óriens ex alto:

Illumináre his, qui in ténebris, et in umbra mortis sedent: * ad dirigéndos pedes nostros in viam pacis.

Canticle of Zacharias

Luke 1:68-79

Blessed be the Lord ✠ God of Israel; * because he hath visited and wrought the redemption of his people:

And hath raised up an horn of salvation to us, * in the house of David his servant:

As he spoke by the mouth of his holy Prophets, * who are from the beginning:

Salvation from our enemies, * and from the hand of all that hate us:

To perform mercy to our fathers, * and to remember his holy testament,

The oath, which he swore to Abraham our father, * that he would grant to us,

That being delivered from the hand of our enemies, * we may serve him without fear,

In holiness and justice before him, * all our days.

And thou, child, shalt be called the prophet of the Highest: * for thou shalt go before the face of the Lord to prepare his ways:

To give knowledge of salvation to his people, * unto the remission of their sins:

Through the bowels of the mercy of our God, * in which the Orient from on high hath visited us:

To enlighten them that sit in darkness, and in the shadow of death: * to direct our feet into the way of peace.

Tuesday - Lauds

Ant. Eréxit nobis Dóminus cornu salútis in domo David púeri sui.

Kýrie, eléison. Christe, eléison. Kýrie, eléison.

Pater noster, qui es in cælis, sanctificétur nomen tuum: advéniat regnum tuum: fiat volúntas tua, sicut in cælo et in terra. Panem nostrum cotidiánum da nobis hódie: et dimítte nobis débita nostra, sicut et nos dimíttimus debitóribus nostris:
℣. Et ne nos indúcas in tentatiónem:
℟. Sed líbera nos a malo.
℣. Dóminus vobíscum.
℟. Et cum spíritu tuo.
℣. Benedicámus Dómino.
℟. Deo grátias.
℣. Fidélium ánimæ per misericórdiam Dei requiéscant in pace.
℟. Amen.
℣. Divínum auxílium máneat semper nobíscum.
℟. Et cum frátribus nostris abséntibus. Amen.

Ant. The Lord has raised up a horn of salvation for us in the house of David his servant.

Lord have mercy upon us, Christ have mercy upon us, Lord have mercy upon us

Our Father, who art in heaven, Hallowed be thy name. Thy kingdom come. Thy will be done on earth as it is in heaven. Give us this day our daily bread. And forgive us our trespasses, as we forgive those who trespass against us.
℣. And lead us not into temptation:
℟. But deliver us from evil.
℣. The Lord be with you.
℟. And with your spirit.
℣. Let us bless the Lord.
℟. Thanks be to God.
℣. May the souls of the faithful, through the mercy of God, rest in peace.
℟. Amen.
℣. May the divine assistance remain with us always.
℟. And with our brothers, who are absent. Amen.

WEDNESDAY - LAUDS

℣. Deus in adiutórium meum inténde.

℟. Dómine, ad adiuvándum me festína. Glória Patri, et Fílio, * et Spirítui Sancto. Sicut erat in princípio, et nunc, et semper, * et in sǽcula sæculórum. Amen. Allelúia.

Psalmus 66

Deus misereátur nostri, et benedícat nobis: * illúminet vultum suum super nos, et misereátur nostri.

Ut cognoscámus in terra viam tuam, * in ómnibus géntibus salutáre tuum.

Confiteántur tibi pópuli, Deus: * confiteántur tibi pópuli omnes.

Læténtur et exsúltent gentes: † quóniam iúdicas pópulos in æquitáte, * et gentes in terra dírigis.

Confiteántur tibi pópuli, Deus, † confiteántur tibi pópuli omnes: * terra dedit fructum suum.

Benedícat nos Deus, Deus noster, benedícat nos Deus: * et métuant eum omnes fines terræ.

Glória Patri, et Fílio, * et Spirítui Sancto.

℣. O God, come to my assistance;

℟. O Lord, make haste to help me. Glory be to the Father, and to the Son, * and to the Holy Ghost. As it was in the beginning, is now, * and ever shall be, world without end. Amen. Alleluia.

Psalm 66

May God have mercy on us, and bless us: * may he cause the light of his countenance to shine upon us, and may he have mercy on us.

That we may know thy way upon earth: * thy salvation in all nations.

Let people confess to thee, O God: * let all people give praise to thee.

Let the nations be glad and rejoice: † for thou judgest the people with justice, * and directest the nations upon earth.

Let the people, O God, confess to thee: † let all the people give praise to thee: * the earth hath yielded her fruit.

May God, our God bless us, may God bless us: * and all the ends of the earth fear him.

Glory be to the Father, and to the Son, * and to the Holy Ghost.

Wednesday - Lauds

Sicut erat in princípio, et nunc, et semper, * et in sǽcula sæculórum. Amen.

Per annum, Ant. Amplius lava me, † Dómine ab iniustítia mea.

Tempore paschali, Ant. Allelúia, † allelúia, allelúia.

Et dicitur tres psalmi sequentes sub una antiphona.

Psalmus 50 [1]

MISERÉRE mei, Deus, * secúndum magnam misericórdiam tuam.

Et secúndum multitúdinem miseratiónum tuárum, * dele iniquitátem meam.

Amplius lava me ab iniquitáte mea: * et a peccáto meo munda me.

Quóniam iniquitátem meam ego cognósco: * et peccátum meum contra me est semper.

Tibi soli peccávi, et malum coram te feci: * ut iustificéris in sermónibus tuis, et vincas cum iudicáris.

Ecce enim, in iniquitátibus concéptus sum: * et in peccátis concépit me mater mea.

Ecce enim, veritátem dilexísti: * incérta et occúlta sapiéntiæ tuæ manifestásti mihi.

Aspérges me hyssópo, et mundábor: * lavábis me, et super nivem dealbábor.

Audítui meo dabis gáudium et lætítiam: * et exsultábunt ossa humiliáta.

As it was in the beginning, is now, * and ever shall be, world without end. Amen.

During the year, Ant. Wash me yet more, O Lord † from my iniquity.

Paschaltide, Ant. Alleluia, † alleluia, alleluia.

And the three following psalms are said under this one antiphon.

Psalm 50 [1]

HAVE mercy on me, O God, * according to thy great mercy.

And according to the multitude of thy tender mercies * blot out my iniquity.

Wash me yet more from my iniquity, * and cleanse me from my sin.

For I know my iniquity, * and my sin is always before me.

To thee only have I sinned, and have done evil before thee: * that thou mayst be justified in thy words, and mayst overcome when thou art judged.

For behold I was conceived in iniquities; * and in sins did my mother conceive me.

For behold thou hast loved truth: * the uncertain and hidden things of thy wisdom thou hast made manifest to me.

Thou shalt sprinkle me with hyssop, and I shall be cleansed: * thou shalt wash me, and I shall be made whiter than snow.

To my hearing thou shalt give joy and gladness: * and the bones

Avérte fáciem tuam a peccátis meis: * et omnes iniquitátes meas dele.

Cor mundum crea in me, Deus: * et spíritum rectum ínnova in viscéribus meis.

Ne proícias me a fácie tua: * et spíritum sanctum tuum ne áuferas a me.

Redde mihi lætítiam salutáris tui: * et spíritu principáli confírma me.

Docébo iníquos vias tuas: * et ímpii ad te converténtur.

Líbera me de sanguínibus, Deus, Deus salútis meæ: * et exsultábit lingua mea iustítiam tuam.

Dómine, lábia mea apéries: * et os meum annuntiábit laudem tuam.

Quóniam si voluísses sacrifícium, dedíssem útique: * holocáustis non delectáberis.

Sacrifícium Deo spíritus contribulátus: * cor contrítum, et humiliátum, Deus, non despícies.

Benígne fac, Dómine, in bona voluntáte tua Sion: * ut ædificéntur muri Ierúsalem.

Tunc acceptábis sacrifícium iustítiæ, oblatiónes, et holocáusta: * tunc impónent super altáre tuum vítulos.

that have been humbled shall rejoice.

Turn away thy face from my sins, * and blot out all my iniquities.

Create a clean heart in me, O God: * and renew a right spirit within my bowels.

Cast me not away from thy face; * and take not thy holy spirit from me.

Restore unto me the joy of thy salvation, * and strengthen me with a perfect spirit.

I will teach the unjust thy ways: * and the wicked shall be converted to thee.

Deliver me from blood, O God, thou God of my salvation: * and my tongue shall extol thy justice.

O Lord, thou wilt open my lips: * and my mouth shall declare thy praise.

For if thou hadst desired sacrifice, I would indeed have given it: * with burnt offerings thou wilt not be delighted.

A sacrifice to God is an afflicted spirit: * a contrite and humbled heart, O God, thou wilt not despise.

Deal favourably, O Lord, in thy good will with Sion; * that the walls of Jerusalem may be built up.

Then shalt thou accept the sacrifice of justice, oblations and whole burnt offerings: * then shall they lay calves upon thy altar.

Wednesday - Lauds

Ant. Amplius lava me, Dómine ab iniustítia mea.

Ant. A timóre † inimíci éripe, Dómine ánimam meam.

Psalmus 63 [2]

EXÁUDI, Deus, oratiónem meam cum déprecor: * a timóre inimíci éripe ánimam meam.

Protexísti me a convéntu malignántium: * a multitúdine operántium iniquitátem.

Quia exacuérunt ut gládium linguas suas: † intendérunt arcum rem amáram, * ut sagíttent in occúltis immaculátum.

Súbito sagittábunt eum, et non timébunt: * firmavérunt sibi sermónem nequam.

Narravérunt ut abscónderent láqueos: * dixérunt: Quis vidébit eos?

Scrutáti sunt iniquitátes: * defecérunt scrutántes scrutínio.

Accédet homo ad cor altum: * et exaltábitur Deus.

Sagíttæ parvulórum factæ sunt plagæ eórum: * et infirmátæ sunt contra eos linguæ eórum.

Conturbáti sunt omnes qui vidébant eos: * et tímuit omnis homo.

Et annuntiavérunt ópera Dei, * et facta eius intellexérunt.

Lætábitur iustus in Dómino, et sperábit in eo, * et laudabúntur omnes recti corde.

Ant. Wash me yet more, O Lord from my iniquity.

Ant. From the fear † of the enemy, deliver my soul O Lord.

Psalm 63 [2]

HEAR, O God, my prayer, when I make supplication to thee: * deliver my soul from the fear of the enemy.

Thou hast protected me from the assembly of the malignant; * from the multitude of the workers of iniquity.

For they have whetted their tongues like a sword; † they have bent their bow a bitter thing, * to shoot in secret the undefiled.

They will shoot at him on a sudden, and will not fear: * they are resolute in wickedness.

They have talked of hiding snares; * they have said: Who shall see them?

They have searched after iniquities: * they have failed in their search.

Man shall come to a deep heart: * and God shall be exalted.

The arrows of children are their wounds: * and their tongues against them are made weak.

All that saw them were troubled; * and every man was afraid.

And they declared the works of God: * and understood his doings.

The just shall rejoice in the Lord, and shall hope in him: * and all the upright in heart shall be praised.

Wednesday - Lauds

Ant. A timóre inimíci éripe, Dómine ánimam meam.

Ant. Te décet hymnus, † Deus in Sion.

Psalmus 64 [3]

TE decet hymnus, Deus, in Sion: * et tibi reddétur votum in Ierúsalem.

Exáudi oratiónem meam: * ad te omnis caro véniet.

Verba iniquórum prævaluérunt super nos: * et impietátibus nostris tu propitiáberis.

Beátus, quem elegísti, et assumpsísti: * inhabitábit in átriis tuis.

Replébimur in bonis domus tuæ: * sanctum est templum tuum, mirábile in æquitáte.

Exáudi nos, Deus, salutáris noster, * spes ómnium fínium terræ, et in mari longe.

Præparans montes in virtúte tua, accínctus poténtia: * qui contúrbas profúndum maris sonum flúctuum eius.

Turbabúntur gentes, et timébunt qui hábitant términos a signis tuis: * éxitus matutíni, et véspere delectábis.

Visitásti terram, et inebriásti eam: * multiplicásti locupletáre eam.

Flumen Dei replétum est aquis, † parásti cibum illórum: * quóniam ita est præparátio eius.

Ant. From the fear of the enemy, deliver my soul O Lord.

Ant. A hymn, O God † becometh thee in Sion.

Psalm 64 [3]

A hymn, O God, becometh thee in Sion: * and a vow shall be paid to thee in Jerusalem.

O hear my prayer: * all flesh shall come to thee.

The words of the wicked have prevailed over us: * and thou wilt pardon our transgressions.

Blessed is he whom thou hast chosen and taken to thee: * he shall dwell in thy courts.

We shall be filled with the good things of thy house; holy is thy temple, * wonderful in justice.

Hear us, O God our saviour, * who art the hope of all the ends of the earth, and in the sea afar off.

Thou who preparest the mountains by thy strength, being girded with power: * who troublest the depth of the sea, the noise of its waves.

The Gentiles shall be troubled, and they that dwell in the uttermost borders shall be afraid at thy signs: * thou shalt make the outgoings of the morning and of the evening to be joyful.

Thou hast visited the earth, and hast plentifully watered it; * thou hast many ways enriched it.

The river of God is filled with water, † thou hast prepared their food; * for so is its preparation.

Wednesday - Lauds

Rivos eius inébria, multíplica genímina eius: * in stillicídiis eius lætábitur gérminans.

Benedíces corónæ anni benignitátis tuæ: * et campi tui replebúntur ubertáte.

Pinguéscent speciósa desérti: * et exsultatióne colles accingéntur.

Indúti sunt aríetes óvium, † et valles abundábunt fruménto: * clamábunt, étenim hymnum dicent.
Per annum, Ant. Te décet hymnus, Deus in Sion.
Tempore paschali, Ant. Allelúia, allelúia, allelúia.

Canticum Feriale
Ant. Dóminus † iudicábit fines terræ. (*T.P.* Allelúia.)

Canticum Annæ [4]
I Reg. 2:1-20

EXULTÁVIT cor meum in Dómino, * et exaltátum est cornu meum in Deo meo.

Dilatátum est os meum super inimícos meos: * quia lætáta sum in salutári tuo.

Non est sanctus, ut est Dóminus, † neque enim est álius extra te, * et non est fortis sicut Deus noster.

Nolíte multiplicáre loqui sublímia, * gloriántes;

Fill up plentifully the streams thereof, multiply its fruits; * it shall spring up and rejoice in its showers.

Thou shalt bless the crown of the year of thy goodness: * and thy fields shall be filled with plenty.

The beautiful places of the wilderness shall grow fat: * and the hills shall be girded about with joy.

The rams of the flock are clothed, † and the vales shall abound with corn: * they shall shout, yea they shall sing a hymn.
During the year, Ant. A hymn, O God becometh thee in Sion.
Paschaltide, Ant. Alleluia, alleluia, alleluia.

Ferial Canticle
Ant. The Lord † will judge the ends of the earth. (*P.T.* Alleluia.)

Canticle of Anna [4]
1 Kings 2:1-10

My heart hath rejoiced in the Lord, * and my horn is exalted in my God:

My mouth is enlarged over my enemies: * because I have rejoiced in thy salvation.

There is none holy as the Lord is: † for there is no other beside thee, * and there is none strong like our God.

Do not multiply to speak lofty things, * boasting:

Wednesday - Lauds

Recédant vétera de ore vestro: † quia Deus scientiárum Dóminus est, * et ipsi præparántur cogitatiónes.

Arcus fórtium superátus est, * et infírmi accíncti sunt róbore.

Repléti prius, pro pánibus se locavérunt: * et famélici saturáti sunt.

Donec stérilis péperit plúrimos: * et quæ multos habébat fílios, infirmáta est.

Dóminus mortíficat et vivíficat; * dedúcit ad ínferos et redúcit.

Dóminus páuperem facit et ditat, * humíliat et súblevat.

Súscitat de púlvere egénum, * et de stércore élevat páuperem:

Ut sédeat cum princípibus, * et sólium glóriæ téneat.

Dómini enim sunt cárdines terræ, * et pósuit super eos orbem.

Pedes sanctórum suórum servábit, † et ímpii in ténebris conticéscent: * quia non in fortitúdine sua roborábitur vir.

Dóminum formidábunt adversárii eius: * et super ipsos in cælis tonábit.

Dóminus iudicábit fines terræ, † et dabit impérium regi suo, * et sublimábit cornu Christi sui.

Let old matters depart from your mouth: † for the Lord is a God of all knowledge, * and to him are thoughts prepared.

The bow of the mighty is overcome, * and the weak are girt with strength.

They that were full before have hired out themselves for bread: * and the hungry are filled;

So that the barren hath borne many: * and she that had many children is weakened.

The Lord killeth and maketh alive, * he bringeth down to hell and bringeth back again.

The Lord maketh poor and maketh rich, * he humbleth and he exalteth.

He raiseth up the needy from the dust, * and lifteth up the poor from the dunghill:

That he may sit with princes, * and hold the throne of glory.

For the poles of the earth are the Lord's, * and upon them he hath set the world.

He will keep the feet of his saints, † and the wicked shall be silent in darkness, * because no man shall prevail by his own strength.

The adversaries of the Lord shall fear him: * and upon them shall he thunder in the heavens.

The Lord shall judge the ends of the earth, † and he shall give empire to his king, * and shall exalt the horn of his Christ.

54 — Wednesday - Lauds

Ant. Dóminus iudicábit fines terræ. (*T.P.* Allelúia.)

Canticum Festivum

Ant. Dómine, † magnus es tu et præclárus in virtúte tua. (*T.P.* Allelúia.)

Canticum Iudith [4]
Iudith 16:15-22

HYMNUM cantémus Dómino, * hymnum novum cantémus Deo nostro.

Adonái, Dómine, magnus es tu, † et præclárus in virtúte tua, * et quem superáre nemo potest.

Tibi sérviat omnis creatúra tua: * quia dixísti, et facta sunt:

Misísti spíritum tuum, et creáta sunt, * et non est qui resístat voci tuæ.

Montes a fundaméntis movebúntur cum aquis: * petræ, sicut cera, liquéscent ante fáciem tuam.

Qui autem timent te, * magni erunt apud te per ómnia.

Væ genti insurgénti super genus meum: † Dóminus enim omnípotens vindicábit in eis, * in die iudícii visitábit illos.

Dabit enim ignem, et vermes in carnes eórum, * ut urántur, et séntiant usque in sempitérnum.

Ant. Dómine, magnus es tu et præclárus in virtúte tua.(*T.P.* Allelúia.)

Ant. The Lord will judge the ends of the earth. (*P.T.* Alleluia.)

Festal Canticle

Ant. O Lord, † great art thou and glorious in thy power. (*P.T.* Alleluia.)

Canticle of Judith [4]
Judith 16:15-22

LET us sing a hymn to the Lord, * let us sing a new hymn to our God.

O Adonai, Lord, great art thou, † and glorious in thy power, * and no one can overcome thee.

Let all thy creatures serve thee: * because thou hast spoken, and they were made:

Thou didst send forth thy spirit, and they were created, * and there is no one that can resist thy voice.

The mountains shall be moved from the foundations with the waters: * the rocks shall melt as wax before thy face.

But they that fear thee, * shall be great with thee in all things.

Woe be to the nation that riseth up against my people: † for the Lord almighty will take revenge on them, * in the day of judgment he will visit them.

For he will give fire, and worms into their flesh, * that they may burn, and may feel for ever.

Ant. O Lord, great art thou and glorious in thy power. (*P.T.* Alleluia.)

Wednesday - Lauds

Ant. Cæli cælórum, † laudáte Deum.

Tempore paschali, Ant. Allelúia, † allelúia, allelúia.

Psalmus 148 [5]

Laudáte Dóminum de cælis: * laudáte eum in excélsis.

Laudáte eum, omnes Angeli eius: * laudáte eum, omnes virtútes eius.

Laudáte eum, sol et luna: * laudáte eum, omnes stellæ et lumen.

Laudáte eum, cæli cælórum: * et aquæ omnes, quæ super cælos sunt, laudent nomen Dómini.

Quia ipse dixit, et facta sunt: * ipse mandávit, et creáta sunt.

Státuit ea in ætérnum, et in sǽculum sǽculi: * præcéptum pósuit, et non præteríbit.

Laudáte Dóminum de terra, * dracónes, et omnes abýssi.

Ignis, grando, nix, glácies, spíritus procellárum: * quæ fáciunt verbum eius:

Montes, et omnes colles: * ligna fructífera, et omnes cedri.

Béstiæ, et univérsa pécora: * serpéntes, et vólucres pennátæ:

Reges terræ, et omnes pópuli: * príncipes, et omnes iúdices terræ.

Iúvenes, et vírgines: † senes cum iunióribus laudent nomen

Ant. Ye heavens of heavens † praise the Lord.

Paschaltide, Ant. Alleluia, † alleluia, alleluia.

Psalm 148 [5]

Praise ye the Lord from the heavens * praise ye him in the high places.

Praise ye him, all his angels: * praise ye him, all his hosts.

Praise ye him, O sun and moon: * praise him, all ye stars and light.

Praise him, ye heavens of heavens: * and let all the waters that are above the heavens, praise the name of the Lord.

For he spoke, and they were made: * he commanded, and they were created.

He hath established them for ever, and for ages of ages: * he hath made a decree, and it shall not pass away.

Praise the Lord from the earth, * ye dragons, and all ye deeps:

Fire, hail, snow, ice, stormy winds * which fulfill his word:

Mountains and all hills, * fruitful trees and all cedars:

Beasts and all cattle: * serpents and feathered fowls:

Kings of the earth and all people: * princes and all judges of the earth:

Young men and maidens: † let the old with the younger, praise

56 Wednesday - Lauds

Dómini: * quia exaltátum est nomen eius solíus.

Conféssio eius super cælum et terram: * et exaltávit cornu pópuli sui.

Hymnus ómnibus sanctis eius: * fíliis Israël, pópulo appropinquánti sibi.

Hic non dicitur Gloria Patri.

Psalmus 149 [6]

CANTÁTE Dómino cánticum novum: * laus eius in ecclésia sanctórum.

Lætétur Israël in eo, qui fecit eum: * et fílii Sion exsúltent in rege suo.

Laudent nomen eius in choro: * in týmpano, et psaltério psallant ei:

Quia beneplácitum est Dómino in pópulo suo: * et exaltábit mansuétos in salútem.

Exsultábunt sancti in glória: * lætabúntur in cubílibus suis.

Exaltatiónes Dei in gútture eórum: * et gládii ancípites in mánibus eórum.

Ad faciéndam vindíctam in natiónibus: * increpatiónes in pópulis.

Ad alligándos reges eórum in compédibus: * et nóbiles eórum in mánicis férreis.

Ut fáciant in eis iudícium conscríptum: * glória hæc est ómnibus sanctis eius.

Hic non dicitur Gloria Patri.

the name of the Lord: * For his name alone is exalted.

The praise of him is above heaven and earth: * and he hath exalted the horn of his people.

A hymn to all his saints: to the children of Israel, a people approaching him.

Here the Glory be is not said.

Psalm 149 [6]

SING ye to the Lord a new canticle: * let his praise be in the church of the saints.

Let Israel rejoice in him that made him: * and let the children of Sion be joyful in their king.

Let them praise his name in choir: * let them sing to him with the timbrel and the psaltery.

For the Lord is well pleased with his people: * and he will exalt the meek unto salvation.

The saints shall rejoice in glory: * they shall be joyful in their beds.

The high praises of God shall be in their mouth: * and twoedged swords in their hands:

To execute vengeance upon the nations, * chastisements among the people:

To bind their kings with fetters, * and their nobles with manacles of iron.

To execute upon them the judgment that is written: * this glory is to all his saints.

Here the Glory be is not said.

Wednesday - Lauds

Psalmus 150 [7]

LAUDÁTE Dóminum in sanctis eius: * laudáte eum in firmaménto virtútis eius.

Laudáte eum in virtútibus eius: * laudáte eum secúndum multitúdinem magnitúdinis eius.

Laudáte eum in sono tubæ: * laudáte eum in psaltério, et cíthara.

Laudáte eum in týmpano, et choro: * laudáte eum in chordis, et órgano.

Laudáte eum in cýmbalis benesonántibus: † laudáte eum in cýmbalis iubilatiónis: * omnis spíritus laudet Dóminum.

Glória Patri, et Fílio, * et Spirítui Sancto.

Sicut erat in princípio, et nunc, et semper, * et in sǽcula sæculórum. Amen.

Ant. Cæli cælórum, laudáte Deum.

Tempore paschali, Ant. Allelúia, allelúia, allelúia.

Capitulum Rom. 13:12-13

NOX præcéssit, dies autem appropinquávit. † Abiciámus ergo ópera tenebrárum, et induámur arma lucis. * Sicut in die honéste ambulémus.

℟. Deo grátias.

℟.br. Sana ánimam meam, * quia peccávi tibi.

℟. Sana ánimam meam, * quia peccávi tibi.

Psalm 150 [7]

PRAISE ye the Lord in his holy places: * praise ye him in the firmament of his power.

Praise ye him for his mighty acts: * praise ye him according to the multitude of his greatness.

Praise him with sound of trumpet: * praise him with psaltery and harp.

Praise him with timbrel and choir: * praise him with strings and organs.

Praise him on high sounding cymbals: † praise him on cymbals of joy: * let every spirit praise the Lord.

Glory be to the Father, and to the Son, * and to the Holy Ghost.

As it was in the beginning, is now, * and ever shall be, world without end. Amen.

Ant. Ye heavens of heavens praise the Lord.

Paschaltide, Ant. Alleluia, alleluia, alleluia.

Chapter Rom. 13:12-13

THE night is passed, and the day is at hand. Let us therefore cast off the works of darkness, and put on the armour of light. Let us walk honestly, as in the day.

℟. Thanks be to God.

℟.br. Heal my soul, * for I have sinned against thee.

℟. Heal my soul, * for I have sinned against thee.

Wednesday - Lauds

℣. Ego dixi: Dómine, miserére mei

℟. Quia peccávi tibi.

℣. Glória Patri, et Fílio, * et Spirítui Sancto.

℟. Sana ánimam meam, * quia peccávi tibi.

Hymnus

Nox, et tenébræ, et núbila,
Confúsa mundi et túrbida:
Lux intrat, albéscit polus:
Christus venit: discédite.

Calígo terræ scínditur
Percússa solis spículo,
Rebúsque iam color redit,
Vultu niténtis síderis.

Te, Christe, solum nóvimus:
Te mente pura et símplici,
Flendo et canéndo quǽsumus,
Inténde nostris sénsibus.

Sunt multa fucis íllita,
Quæ luce purgéntur tua:
Tu, lux Eói síderis,
Vultu seréno illúmina.

Deo Patri sit glória,
Eiúsque soli Fílio,
Cum Spíritu Paráclito,
Et nunc et in perpétuum.
Amen.

℣. Repléti sumus mane misericórdia tua.

℟. Exsultávimus, et delectáti sumus.

℣. I said: O Lord, be thou merciful to me

℟. For I have sinned against thee.

℣. Glory be to the Father, and to the Son, * and to the Holy Ghost.

℟. Heal my soul, * for I have sinned against thee.

Hymn

Day is breaking, dawn is bright:
Hence, vain shadows of the night!
Mists that dim our mortal sight,
Christ is come! Depart!

Darkness routed lifts her wings
As the radiance upwards springs:
Through the world of wakened things
Life and colour dart.

Thee, O Christ, alone we know:
Singing even in our woe,
With pure hearts to thee we go:
On our senses shine!

In thy beams be purged away
All that leads our thoughts astray!
Through our spirits, King of day,
Pour thy light divine!

All laud to God the Father be;
All praise, Eternal Son, to thee;
All glory, as is ever meet,
To God the Holy Paraclete.
Amen.

℣. We are filled in the morning with thy mercy.

℟. And we have rejoiced, and are delighted.

Wednesday - Lauds

Ant. De manu ómnium † qui odérunt nos, líbera nos Dómine.

Canticum Zachariæ

Luc. 1:68-79

BENEDÍCTUS ✠ Dóminus, Deus Israël: * quia visitávit, et fecit redemptiónem plebis suæ:

Et eréxit cornu salútis nobis: * in domo David, púeri sui.

Sicut locútus est per os sanctórum, * qui a sǽculo sunt, prophetárum eius:
Salútem ex inimícis nostris, * et de manu ómnium, qui odérunt nos.
Ad faciéndam misericórdiam cum pátribus nostris: * et memorári testaménti sui sancti.
Iusiurándum, quod iurávit ad Abraham patrem nostrum, * datúrum se nobis:
Ut sine timóre, de manu inimicórum nostrórum liberáti, * serviámus illi.
In sanctitáte, et iustítia coram ipso, * ómnibus diébus nostris.
Et tu, puer, Prophéta Altíssimi vocáberis: * præíbis enim ante fáciem Dómini, paráre vias eius:

Ad dandam sciéntiam salútis plebi eius: * in remissiónem peccatórum eórum:
Per víscera misericórdiæ Dei nostri: * in quibus visitávit nos, óriens ex alto:
Illumináre his, qui in ténebris, et in umbra mortis sedent: * ad

Ant. From the hand of all † who hate us, the Lord has delivered us.

Canticle of Zacharias

Luke 1:68-79

Blessed be the Lord ✠ God of Israel; * because he hath visited and wrought the redemption of his people:

And hath raised up an horn of salvation to us, * in the house of David his servant:

As he spoke by the mouth of his holy Prophets, * who are from the beginning:
Salvation from our enemies, * and from the hand of all that hate us:
To perform mercy to our fathers, * and to remember his holy testament,
The oath, which he swore to Abraham our father, * that he would grant to us,
That being delivered from the hand of our enemies, * we may serve him without fear,
In holiness and justice before him, * all our days.
And thou, child, shalt be called the prophet of the Highest: * for thou shalt go before the face of the Lord to prepare his ways:
To give knowledge of salvation to his people, * unto the remission of their sins:
Through the bowels of the mercy of our God, * in which the Orient from on high hath visited us:
To enlighten them that sit in darkness, and in the shadow of

Wednesday - Lauds

dirigéndos pedes nostros in viam pacis.

Ant. De manu ómnium qui odérunt nos, líbera nos Dómine.

Kýrie, eléison. Christe, eléison. Kýrie, eléison.

Pater noster, qui es in cælis, sanctificétur nomen tuum: advéniat regnum tuum: fiat volúntas tua, sicut in cælo et in terra. Panem nostrum cotidiánum da nobis hódie: et dimítte nobis débita nostra, sicut et nos dimíttimus debitóribus nostris:

℣. Et ne nos indúcas in tentatiónem:

℟. Sed líbera nos a malo.

℣. Dóminus vobíscum.

℟. Et cum spíritu tuo.

℣. Benedicámus Dómino.

℟. Deo grátias.

℣. Fidélium ánimæ per misericórdiam Dei requiéscant in pace.

℟. Amen.

℣. Divínum auxílium máneat semper nobíscum.

℟. Et cum frátribus nostris abséntibus. Amen.

death: * to direct our feet into the way of peace.

Ant. From the hand of all who hate us, the Lord has delivered us.

Lord have mercy upon us, Christ have mercy upon us, Lord have mercy upon us

Our Father, who art in heaven, Hallowed be thy name. Thy kingdom come. Thy will be done on earth as it is in heaven. Give us this day our daily bread. And forgive us our trespasses, as we forgive those who trespass against us.

℣. And lead us not into temptation:

℟. But deliver us from evil.

℣. The Lord be with you.

℟. And with your spirit.

℣. Let us bless the Lord.

℟. Thanks be to God.

℣. May the souls of the faithful, through the mercy of God, rest in peace.

℟. Amen.

℣. May the divine assistance remain with us always.

℟. And with our brothers, who are absent. Amen.

THURSDAY - LAUDS

℣. Deus in adiutórium meum inténde.

℟. Dómine, ad adiuvándum me festína. Glória Patri, et Fílio, * et Spirítui Sancto. Sicut erat in princípio, et nunc, et semper, * et in sǽcula sæculórum. Amen. Allelúia.

Psalmus 66

DEUS misereátur nostri, et benedícat nobis: * illúminet vultum suum super nos, et misereátur nostri.

Ut cognoscámus in terra viam tuam, * in ómnibus géntibus salutáre tuum.
Confiteántur tibi pópuli, Deus: * confiteántur tibi pópuli omnes.

Læt023ntur et exsúltent gentes: † quóniam iúdicas pópulos in æquitáte, * et gentes in terra dírigis.
Confiteántur tibi pópuli, Deus, † confiteántur tibi pópuli omnes: * terra dedit fructum suum.

Benedícat nos Deus, Deus noster, benedícat nos Deus: * métuant eum omnes fines terræ.
Glória Patri, et Fílio, * et Spirítui Sancto.

℣. O God, come to my assistance;

℟. O Lord, make haste to help me. Glory be to the Father, and to the Son, * and to the Holy Ghost. As it was in the beginning, is now, * and ever shall be, world without end. Amen. Alleluia.

Psalm 66

MAY God have mercy on us, and bless us: * may he cause the light of his countenance to shine upon us, and may he have mercy on us.

That we may know thy way upon earth: * thy salvation in all nations.

Let people confess to thee, O God: * let all people give praise to thee.

Let the nations be glad and rejoice: † for thou judgest the people with justice, * and directest the nations upon earth.

Let the people, O God, confess to thee: † let all the people give praise to thee: * the earth hath yielded her fruit.

May God, our God bless us, may God bless us: * and all the ends of the earth fear him.

Glory be to the Father, and to the Son, * and to the Holy Ghost.

Thursday - Lauds

Sicut erat in princípio, et nunc, et semper, * et in sǽcula sæculórum. Amen.

Per annum, Ant. Tibi soli † peccávi, Dómine, miserére mei.

Tempore paschali, Ant. Allelúia, † allelúia, allelúia.

Et dicitur tres psalmi sequentes sub una antiphona.

Psalmus 50 [1]

MISERÉRE mei, Deus, * secúndum magnam misericórdiam tuam.

Et secúndum multitúdinem miseratiónum tuárum, * dele iniquitátem meam.

Amplius lava me ab iniquitáte mea: * et a peccáto meo munda me.

Quóniam iniquitátem meam ego cognósco: * et peccátum meum contra me est semper.

Tibi soli peccávi, et malum coram te feci: * ut iustificéris in sermónibus tuis, et vincas cum iudicáris.

Ecce enim, in iniquitátibus concéptus sum: * et in peccátis concépit me mater mea.

Ecce enim, veritátem dilexísti: * incérta et occúlta sapiéntiæ tuæ manifestásti mihi.

Aspérges me hyssópo, et mundábor: * lavábis me, et super nivem dealbábor.

Audítui meo dabis gáudium et lætítiam: * et exsultábunt ossa humiliáta.

As it was in the beginning, is now, * and ever shall be, world without end. Amen.

During the year, Ant. Before thee only † have I sinned, O Lord, have mercy on me.

Paschaltide, Ant. Alleluia, † alleluia, alleluia.

And the three following psalms are said under this one antiphon.

Psalm 50 [1]

HAVE mercy on me, O God, * according to thy great mercy.

And according to the multitude of thy tender mercies * blot out my iniquity.

Wash me yet more from my iniquity, * and cleanse me from my sin.

For I know my iniquity, * and my sin is always before me.

To thee only have I sinned, and have done evil before thee: * that thou mayst be justified in thy words, and mayst overcome when thou art judged.

For behold I was conceived in iniquities; * and in sins did my mother conceive me.

For behold thou hast loved truth: * the uncertain and hidden things of thy wisdom thou hast made manifest to me.

Thou shalt sprinkle me with hyssop, and I shall be cleansed: * thou shalt wash me, and I shall be made whiter than snow.

To my hearing thou shalt give joy and gladness: * and the bones

Thursday - Lauds

Avérte fáciem tuam a peccátis meis: * et omnes iniquitátes meas dele.

Cor mundum crea in me, Deus: * et spíritum rectum ínnova in viscéribus meis.

Ne proícias me a fácie tua: * et spíritum sanctum tuum ne áuferas a me.

Redde mihi lætítiam salutáris tui: * et spíritu principáli confírma me.

Docébo iníquos vias tuas: * et ímpii ad te converténtur.

Líbera me de sanguínibus, Deus, Deus salútis meæ: * et exsultábit lingua mea iustítiam tuam.

Dómine, lábia mea apéries: * et os meum annuntiábit laudem tuam.

Quóniam si voluísses sacrifícium, dedíssem útique: * holocáustis non delectáberis.

Sacrifícium Deo spíritus contribulátus: * cor contrítum, et humiliátum, Deus, non despícies.

Benígne fac, Dómine, in bona voluntáte tua Sion: * ut ædificéntur muri Ierúsalem.

Tunc acceptábis sacrifícium iustítiæ, oblatiónes, et holocáusta: * tunc impónent super altáre tuum vítulos.

that have been humbled shall rejoice.

Turn away thy face from my sins, * and blot out all my iniquities.

Create a clean heart in me, O God: * and renew a right spirit within my bowels.

Cast me not away from thy face; * and take not thy holy spirit from me.

Restore unto me the joy of thy salvation, * and strengthen me with a perfect spirit.

I will teach the unjust thy ways: * and the wicked shall be converted to thee.

Deliver me from blood, O God, thou God of my salvation: * and my tongue shall extol thy justice.

O Lord, thou wilt open my lips: * and my mouth shall declare thy praise.

For if thou hadst desired sacrifice, I would indeed have given it: * with burnt offerings thou wilt not be delighted.

A sacrifice to God is an afflicted spirit: * a contrite and humbled heart, O God, thou wilt not despise.

Deal favourably, O Lord, in thy good will with Sion; * that the walls of Jerusalem may be built up.

Then shalt thou accept the sacrifice of justice, oblations and whole burnt offerings: * then shall they lay calves upon thy altar.

64 Thursday - Lauds

Ant. Tibi soli peccávi, Dómine, miserére mei.

Ant. Intret † orátio mea, in conspéctu tuo, Dómine.

Psalmus 87 [2]

DÓMINE, Deus salútis meæ: * in die clamávi, et nocte coram te.

Intret in conspéctu tuo orátio mea: * inclína aurem tuam ad precem meam:

Quia repléta est malis ánima mea: * et vita mea inférno appropinquávit.

Æstimátus sum cum descendéntibus in lacum: * factus sum sicut homo sine adiutório, inter mórtuos liber.

Sicut vulneráti dormiéntes in sepúlcris, † quorum non es memor ámplius: * et ipsi de manu tua repúlsi sunt.

Posuérunt me in lacu inferióri: * in tenebrósis, et in umbra mortis.

Super me confirmátus est furor tuus: * et omnes fluctus tuos induxísti super me.

Longe fecísti notos meos a me: * posuérunt me abominatiónem sibi.

Tráditus sum, et non egrediébar: * óculi mei languérunt præ inópia.

Clamávi ad te, Dómine, tota die: * expándi ad te manus meas.

Ant. Before thee only have I sinned, O Lord, have mercy on me.

Ant. Let my prayer † come in before thee.

Psalm 87 [2]

LORD, the God of my salvation: * I have cried in the day, and in the night before thee.

Let my prayer come in before thee: * incline thy ear to my petition.

For my soul is filled with evils: * and my life hath drawn nigh to hell.

I am counted among them that go down to the pit: * I am become as a man without help, free among the dead.

Like the slain sleeping in the sepulchres, † whom thou rememberest no more: * and they are cast off from thy hand.

They have laid me in the lower pit: * in the dark places, and in the shadow of death.

Thy wrath is strong over me: * and all thy waves thou hast brought in upon me.

Thou hast put away my acquaintance far from me: * they have set me an abomination to themselves.

I was delivered up, and came not forth: * my eyes languished through poverty.

All the day I cried to thee, O Lord: * I stretched out my hands to thee.

Thursday - Lauds 65

Numquid mórtuis fácies mirabília: * aut médici suscitábunt, et confitebúntur tibi?

Numquid narrábit áliquis in sepúlcro misericórdiam tuam, * et veritátem tuam in perditióne?

Numquid cognoscéntur in ténebris mirabília tua, * et iustítia tua in terra obliviónis?

Et ego ad te, Dómine, clamávi: * et mane orátio mea prævéniet te.

Ut quid, Dómine, repéllis oratiónem meam: * avértis fáciem tuam a me?

Pauper sum ego, et in labóribus a iuventúte mea: * exaltátus autem, humiliátus sum et conturbátus.

In me transiérunt iræ tuæ: * et terróres tui conturbavérunt me.

Circumdedérunt me sicut aqua tota die: * circumdedérunt me simul.

Elongásti a me amícum et próximum: * et notos meos a miséria.

Ant. Intret orátio mea, in conspéctu tuo, Dómine.

Ant. Dómine, † refúgium factus es nobis.

Et non repetitur in psalmo.

Psalmus 89 [3]

DÓMINE, refúgium factus es nobis: * a generatióne in generatiónem.

Priúsquam montes fíerent, aut formarétur terra et orbis: * a

Wilt thou shew wonders to the dead? * or shall physicians raise to life, and give praise to thee?

Shall any one in the sepulchre declare thy mercy: * and thy truth in destruction?

Shall thy wonders be known in the dark; * and thy justice in the land of forgetfulness?

But I, O Lord, have cried to thee: * and in the morning my prayer shall prevent thee.

Lord, why castest thou off my prayer: * why turnest thou away thy face from me?

I am poor, and in labours from my youth: * and being exalted have been humbled and troubled.

Thy wrath hath come upon me: * and thy terrors have troubled me.

They have come round about me like water all the day: * they have compassed me about together.

Friend and neighbour thou hast put far from me: * and my acquaintance, because of misery.

Ant. Let my prayer come in before thee.

Ant. Lord, † thou hast been our refuge.

The antiphon is not repeated in the psalm.

Psalm 89 [3]

LORD, thou hast been our refuge * from generation to generation.

Before the mountains were made, or the earth and the world

66 Thursday - Lauds

sǽculo et usque in sǽculum tu es, Deus.

Ne avértas hóminem in humilitátem: * et dixísti: Convertímini, fílii hóminum.

Quóniam mille anni ante óculos tuos, * tamquam dies hestérna, quæ prætériit,

Et custódia in nocte, * quæ pro níhilo habéntur, eórum anni erunt.

Mane sicut herba tránseat, † mane flóreat, et tránseat: * véspere décidat, indúret et aréscat.

Quia defécimus in ira tua, * et in furóre tuo turbáti sumus.

Posuísti iniquitátes nostras in conspéctu tuo: * sǽculum nostrum in illuminatióne vultus tui.

Quóniam omnes dies nostri defecérunt: * et in ira tua defécimus.

Anni nostri sicut aránea meditabúntur: * dies annórum nostrórum in ipsis, septuagínta anni.

Si autem in potentátibus, octogínta anni: * et ámplius eórum, labor et dolor.

Quóniam supervénit mansuetúdo: * et corripiémur.

Quis novit potestátem iræ tuæ: * et præ timóre tuo iram tuam dinumeráre?

Déxteram tuam sic notam fac: * et erudítos corde in sapiéntia.

was formed; * from eternity and to eternity thou art God.

Turn not man away to be brought low: * and thou hast said: Be converted, O ye sons of men.

For a thousand years in thy sight * are as yesterday, which is past.

And as a watch in the night, * things that are counted nothing, shall their years be.

In the morning man shall grow up like grass; † in the morning he shall flourish and pass away: * in the evening he shall fall, grow dry, and wither.

For in thy wrath we have fainted away: * and are troubled in thy indignation.

Thou hast set our iniquities before thy eyes: * our life in the light of thy countenance.

For all our days are spent; * and in thy wrath we have fainted away.

Our years shall be considered as a spider: * the days of our years in them are threescore and ten years.

But if in the strong they be fourscore years: * and what is more of them is labour and sorrow.

For mildness is come upon us: * and we shall be corrected.

Who knoweth the power of thy anger, * and for thy fear can number thy wrath?

So make thy right hand known: * and men learned in heart, in wisdom.

Thursday - Lauds

Convértere, Dómine, úsque-quo? * et deprecábilis esto super servos tuos.

Repléti sumus mane misericórdia tua: * et exsultávimus, et delectáti sumus ómnibus diébus nostris.

Lætáti sumus pro diébus, quibus nos humiliásti: * annis, quibus vídimus mala.

Réspice in servos tuos, et in ópera tua: * et dírige fílios eórum.

Et sit splendor Dómini, Dei nostri, super nos, † et ópera mánuum nostrárum dírige super nos: * et opus mánuum nostrárum dírige.

Per annum, Ant. Dómine, refúgium factus es nobis.

Tempore paschali, Ant. Allelúia, allelúia, allelúia.

Canticum Feriale

Ant. Cantémus † Dómino glorióse. (*T.P.* Allelúia.)

Et non repetitur in cántico.

Canticum Moysi [4]

Exod. 15:1-19

CANTÉMUS Dómino: glorióse enim magnificátus est, * equum et ascensórem deiécit in mare.

Fortitúdo mea, et laus mea Dóminus, * et factus est mihi in salútem:

Return, O Lord, how long? * and be entreated in favour of thy servants.

We are filled in the morning with thy mercy: * and we have rejoiced, and are delighted all our days.

We have rejoiced for the days in which thou hast humbled us: * for the years in which we have seen evils.

Look upon thy servants and upon their works: * and direct their children.

And let the brightness of the Lord our God be upon us: † and direct thou the works of our hands over us; * yea, the work of our hands do thou direct.

During the year, Ant. Lord, thou hast been our refuge.

Paschaltide, Ant. Alleluia, alleluia, alleluia.

Ferial Canticle

Ant. Let us sing † to the Lord gloriously. (*P.T.* Alleluia.)

It is not repeated in the canticle.

Canticle of Moses [4]

Exod. 15:1-19

LET us sing to the Lord: for he is gloriously magnified, * the horse and the rider he hath thrown into the sea.

The Lord is my strength and my praise, * and he is become salvation to me:

Iste Deus meus, et glorificábo eum: * Deus patris mei, et exaltábo eum.

Dóminus quasi vir pugnátor, † Omnípotens nomen eius. * Currus Pharaónis et exércitum eius proiécit in mare:

Elécti príncipes eius submérsi sunt in mari Rubro. † Abýssi operuérunt eos; * descendérunt in profúndum quasi lapis.

Déxtera tua, Dómine, magnificáta est in fortitúdine: † déxtera tua, Dómine, percússit inimícum. * Et in multitúdine glóriæ tuæ deposuísti adversários tuos:

Misísti iram tuam, quæ devorávit eos sicut stípulam. * Et in spíritu furóris tui congregátæ sunt aquæ:

Stetit unda fluens, * congregáta sunt abýssi in médio mari.

Dixit inimícus: Pérsequar et compréhendam, * díividam spólia, implébitur ánima mea:

Evaginábo gládium meum, * interfíciet eos manus mea.

Flavit spíritus tuus, et opéruit eos mare: * submérsi sunt quasi plumbum in aquis veheméntibus.

Quis símilis tui in fórtibus, Dómine? † quis símilis tui, magníficus in sanctitáte, * terríbilis atque laudábilis, fáciens mirabília?

He is my God and I will glorify him: * the God of my father, and I will exalt him.

The Lord is as a man of war, † Almighty is his name. * Pharao's chariots and his army he hath cast into the sea:

His chosen captains are drowned in the Red Sea. † The depths have covered them, * they are sunk to the bottom like a stone.

Thy right hand, O Lord, is magnified in strength: † thy right hand, O Lord, hath slain the enemy. * And in the multitude of thy glory thou hast put down thy adversaries:

Thou hast sent thy wrath, which hath devoured them like stubble. * And with the blast of thy anger the waters were gathered together:

The flowing water stood, * the depths were gathered together in the midst of the sea.

The enemy said: I will pursue and overtake, * I will divide the spoils, my soul shall have its fill:

I will draw my sword, * my hand shall slay them.

Thy wind blew and the sea covered them: * they sunk as lead in the mighty waters.

Who is like to thee, among the strong, O Lord? † who is like to thee, glorious in holiness, * terrible and praiseworthy, doing wonders?

Thursday - Lauds

Extendísti manum tuam, et devorábit eos terra. * Dux fuísti in misericórdia tua pópulo quem redemísti:

Et portásti eum in fortitúdine tua, * ad habitáculum sanctum tuum.

Ascendérunt pópuli, et iráti sunt: * dolóres obtinuérunt habitatóres Philísthiim.

Tunc conturbáti sunt príncipes Edom, † robústos Moab obtínuit tremor: * obriguérunt omnes habitátores Chánaan.

Irruat super eos formído et pavor, * in magnitúdine bráchii tui:

Fiant immóbiles quasi lapis, † donec pertránseat pópulus tuus, Dómine, * donec pertránseat pópulus tuus iste, quem possedísti.

Introdúces eos, et plantábis in monte hæreditátis tuæ, * firmíssimo habitáculo tuo quod operátus es, Dómine:

Sanctuárium tuum, Dómine, quod firmavérunt manus tuæ. * Dóminus regnábit in ætérnum et ultra.

Ingréssus est enim eques Phárao cum cúrribus et equítibus eius in mare: * et redúxit super eos Dóminus aquas maris:

Fílii autem Israël ambulavérunt per siccum * in médio eius.

Thou stretchedst forth thy hand, and the earth swallowed them. * In thy mercy thou hast been a leader to the people which thou hast redeemed:

And in thy strength thou hast carried them * to thy holy habitation.

Nations rose up, and were angry: * sorrows took hold on the inhabitants of Philisthiim.

Then were the princes of Edom troubled, † trembling seized on the stout men of Moab: * all the inhabitants of Chanaan became stiff.

Let fear and dread fall upon them, * in the greatness of thy arm:

Let them become unmoveable as a stone, † until thy people, O Lord, pass by: * until this thy people pass by, which thou hast possessed.

Thou shalt bring them in, and plant them in the mountain of thy inheritance, * in thy most firm habitation which thou hast made, O Lord;

Thy sanctuary, O Lord, which thy hands have established. * The Lord shall reign for ever and ever.

For Pharao went in on horseback with his chariots and horsemen into the sea: * and the Lord brought back upon them the waters of the sea:

But the children of Israel walked on dry ground * in the midst thereof.

Thursday - Lauds

Ant. Cantémus Dómino gloróse. (*T.P.* Allelúia.)

Ant. Let us sing to the Lord gloriously. (*P.T.* Alleluia.)

Canticum Festivum

Ant. Pópulus meus, † ait Dóminus, bonis meis adimplébitur. (*T.P.* Allelúia.)

Canticum Ieremiæ [4]

Ier. 31:10-14

Audíte verbum Dómini, gentes, * et annuntiáte in ínsulis, quæ procul sunt,

Et dícite: Qui dispérsit Israël, congregábit eum: * et custódiet eum sicut pastor gregem suum.

Redémit enim Dóminus Iacob, * et liberávit eum de manu potentióris.

Et vénient, et laudábunt in monte Sion: * et cónfluent ad bona Dómini,

Super fruménto, et vino, et óleo, * et fœtu pécorum et armentórum:

Erítque ánima eórum quasi hortus irríguus, * et ultra non esúrient.

Tunc lætábitur virgo in choro, * iúvenes et senes simul:

Et convértam luctum eórum in gáudium, * et consolábor eos, et lætificábo a dolóre suo.

Festal Canticle

Ant. My people † said the Lord, shall be filled with good things. (*P.T.* Alleluia.)

Canticle of Jeremias [4]

Jer. 31:10-14

Hear the word of the Lord, O ye nations, * and declare it in the islands that are afar off,

And say: He that scattered Israel will gather him: * and he will keep him as the shepherd doth his flock.

For the Lord hath redeemed Jacob, * and delivered him out of the hand of one that was mightier than he.

And they shall come, and shall give praise in mount Sion: * and they shall flow together to the good things of the Lord,

For the corn, and wine, and oil, * and the increase of cattle and herds,

And their soul shall be as a watered garden, * and they shall be hungry no more.

Then shall the virgin rejoice in the dance, * the young men and old men together:

And I will turn their mourning into joy, * and will comfort them, and make them joyful after their sorrow.

Et inebriábo ánimam sacerdótum pinguédine: * et pópulus meus bonis meis adimplébitur.

Ant. Pópulus meus, ait Dóminus, bonis meis adimplébitur. (*T.P.* Allelúia.)

Ant. In sanctis eius † laudáte Deum.

Tempore paschali, Ant. Allelúia, † allelúia, allelúia.

Psalmus 148 [5]

Laudáte Dóminum de cælis: * laudáte eum in excélsis.

Laudáte eum, omnes Angeli eius: * laudáte eum, omnes virtútes eius.

Laudáte eum, sol et luna: * laudáte eum, omnes stellæ et lumen.

Laudáte eum, cæli cælórum: * et aquæ omnes, quæ super cælos sunt, laudent nomen Dómini.

Quia ipse dixit, et facta sunt: * ipse mandávit, et creáta sunt.

Státuit ea in ætérnum, et in sǽculum sǽculi: * præcéptum pósuit, et non præteríbit.

Laudáte Dóminum de terra, * dracónes, et omnes abýssi.

Ignis, grando, nix, glácies, spíritus procellárum: * quæ fáciunt verbum eius:

Montes, et omnes colles: * ligna fructífera, et omnes cedri.

And I will fill the soul of the priests with fatness: * and my people shall be filled with my good things.

Ant. My people said the Lord, shall be filled with good things. (*P.T.* Alleluia.)

Ant. Praise ye the Lord † in his holy places.

Paschaltide, Ant. Alleluia, † alleluia, alleluia.

Psalm 148 [5]

Praise ye the Lord from the heavens * praise ye him in the high places.

Praise ye him, all his angels: * praise ye him, all his hosts.

Praise ye him, O sun and moon: * praise him, all ye stars and light.

Praise him, ye heavens of heavens: * and let all the waters that are above the heavens, praise the name of the Lord.

For he spoke, and they were made: * he commanded, and they were created.

He hath established them for ever, and for ages of ages: * he hath made a decree, and it shall not pass away.

Praise the Lord from the earth, * ye dragons, and all ye deeps:

Fire, hail, snow, ice, stormy winds * which fulfill his word:

Mountains and all hills, * fruitful trees and all cedars:

Béstiæ, et univérsa pécora: * serpéntes, et vólucres pennátæ: Reges terræ, et omnes pópuli: * príncipes, et omnes iúdices terræ.

Iúvenes, et vírgines: † senes cum iunióribus laudent nomen Dómini: * quia exaltátum est nomen eius solíus.

Conféssio eius super cælum et terram: * et exaltávit cornu pópuli sui.

Hymnus ómnibus sanctis eius: * fíliis Israël, pópulo appropinquánti sibi.

Hic non dicitur Gloria Patri.

Psalmus 149 [6]

CANTÁTE Dómino cánticum novum: * laus eius in ecclésia sanctórum.

Lætétur Israël in eo, qui fecit eum: * et fílii Sion exsúltent in rege suo.

Laudent nomen eius in choro: * in týmpano, et psaltério psallant ei:

Quia beneplácitum est Dómino in pópulo suo: * et exaltábit mansuétos in salútem.

Exsultábunt sancti in glória: * lætabúntur in cubílibus suis.

Exaltatiónes Dei in gútture eórum: * et gládii ancípites in mánibus eórum.

Ad faciéndam vindíctam in natiónibus: * increpatiónes in pópulis.

Beasts and all cattle: * serpents and feathered fowls:

Kings of the earth and all people: * princes and all judges of the earth:

Young men and maidens: † let the old with the younger, praise the name of the Lord: * For his name alone is exalted.

The praise of him is above heaven and earth: * and he hath exalted the horn of his people.

A hymn to all his saints: to the children of Israel, a people approaching him.

Here the Glory be is not said.

Psalm 149 [6]

SING ye to the Lord a new canticle: * let his praise be in the church of the saints.

Let Israel rejoice in him that made him: * and let the children of Sion be joyful in their king.

Let them praise his name in choir: * let them sing to him with the timbrel and the psaltery.

For the Lord is well pleased with his people: * and he will exalt the meek unto salvation.

The saints shall rejoice in glory: * they shall be joyful in their beds.

The high praises of God shall be in their mouth: * and twoedged swords in their hands:

To execute vengeance upon the nations, * chastisements among the people:

Thursday - Lauds

Ad alligándos reges eórum in compédibus: * et nóbiles eórum in mánicis férreis.

Ut fáciant in eis iudícium conscríptum: * glória hæc est ómnibus sanctis eius.

Hic non dicitur Gloria Patri.

Psalmus 150 [7]

L AUDÁTE Dóminum in sanctis eius: * laudáte eum in firmaménto virtútis eius.

Laudáte eum in virtútibus eius: * laudáte eum secúndum multitúdinem magnitúdinis eius.

Laudáte eum in sono tubæ: * laudáte eum in psaltério, et cíthara.

Laudáte eum in týmpano, et choro: * laudáte eum in chordis, et órgano.

Laudáte eum in cýmbalis benesonántibus: † laudáte eum in cýmbalis iubilatiónis: * omnis spíritus laudet Dóminum.

Glória Patri, et Fílio, * et Spirítui Sancto.

Sicut erat in princípio, et nunc, et semper, * et in sǽcula sæculórum. Amen.

Ant. In sanctis eius laudáte Deum.

Tempore paschali, Ant. Allelúia, allelúia, allelúia.

Capitulum   Rom. 13:12-13

N OX præcéssit, dies autem appropinquávit. † Abiciámus ergo ópera tenebrárum, et induámur arma lucis. * Sicut in die honéste ambulémus.

℟. Deo grátias.

To bind their kings with fetters, * and their nobles with manacles of iron.

To execute upon them the judgment that is written: * this glory is to all his saints.

Here the Glory be is not said.

Psalm 150 [7]

P RAISE ye the Lord in his holy places: * praise ye him in the firmament of his power.

Praise ye him for his mighty acts: * praise ye him according to the multitude of his greatness.

Praise him with sound of trumpet: * praise him with psaltery and harp.

Praise him with timbrel and choir: * praise him with strings and organs.

Praise him on high sounding cymbals: † praise him on cymbals of joy: * let every spirit praise the Lord.

Glory be to the Father, and to the Son, * and to the Holy Ghost.

As it was in the beginning, is now, * and ever shall be, world without end. Amen.

Ant. Praise ye the Lord in his holy places.

Paschaltide, Ant. Alleluia, alleluia, alleluia.

Chapter   Rom. 13:12-13

T HE night is passed, and the day is at hand. Let us therefore cast off the works of darkness, and put on the armour of light. Let us walk honestly, as in the day.

℟. Thanks be to God.

℟.br. Sana ánimam meam, * quia peccávi tibi.
℟. Sana ánimam meam, * quia peccávi tibi.
℣. Ego dixi: Dómine, miserére mei
℟. Quia peccávi tibi.

℣. Glória Patri, et Fílio, * et Spirítui Sancto.

℟. Sana ánimam meam, * quia peccávi tibi.

Hymnus

Lux ecce surgit áurea,
Pallens fatíscat cǽcitas,
Quæ nosmet in præceps diu
Erróre traxit dévio.

Hæc lux serénum cónferat,
Purósque nos præstet sibi:
Nihil loquámur súbdolum:
Volvámus obscúrum nihil.

Sic tota decúrrat dies,
Ne lingua mendax, ne manus
Oculíve peccent lúbrici,
Ne noxa corpus ínquinet.

Speculátor astat désuper,
Qui nos diébus ómnibus,
Actúsque nostros próspicit
A luce prima in vésperum.

Deo Patri sit glória,
Eiúsque soli Fílio,
Cum Spíritu Paráclito,
Et nunc et in perpétuum.
Amen.

℟.br. Heal my soul, * for I have sinned against thee.
℟. Heal my soul, * for I have sinned against thee.
℣. I said: O Lord, be thou merciful to me
℟. For I have sinned against thee.

℣. Glory be to the Father, and to the Son, * and to the Holy Ghost.

℟. Heal my soul, * for I have sinned against thee.

Hymn

See the golden sun arise!
Let no more our darkened eyes
Snare us, tangled by surprise
In the maze of sin!

From false words and thoughts impure
Let this light, serene and sure,
Keep our lips without secure,
Keep our souls within.

So may we the day-time spend,
That, till life's temptations end,
Tongue, nor hand, nor eye offend!
One, above us all,

Views in his revealing ray
All we do, and think, and say,
Watching us from break of day
Till the twilight fall.

All laud to God the Father be;
All praise, Eternal Son, to thee;
All glory, as is ever meet,
To God the Holy Paraclete.
Amen.

Thursday - Lauds

℣. Repléti sumus mane misericórdia tua.

℞. Exsultávimus, et delectáti sumus.

Ant. In sanctitáte † serviámus Dómino, et liberábit nos ab inimícis nostris.

Canticum Zachariæ
Luc. 1:68-79

BENEDÍCTUS ✠ Dóminus, Deus Israël: * quia visitávit, et fecit redemptiónem plebis suæ:

Et eréxit cornu salútis nobis: * in domo David, púeri sui.

Sicut locútus est per os sanctórum, * qui a sǽculo sunt, prophetárum eius:

Salútem ex inimícis nostris, * et de manu ómnium, qui odérunt nos.

Ad faciéndam misericórdiam cum pátribus nostris: * et memorári testaménti sui sancti.

Iusiurándum, quod iurávit ad Abraham patrem nostrum, * datúrum se nobis:

Ut sine timóre, de manu inimicórum nostrórum liberáti, * serviámus illi.

In sanctitáte, et iustítia coram ipso, * ómnibus diébus nostris.

Et tu, puer, Prophéta Altíssimi vocáberis: * præíbis enim ante fáciem Dómini, paráre vias eius:

℣. We are filled in the morning with thy mercy.

℞. And we have rejoiced, and are delighted.

Ant. In holiness † let us serve the Lord, and he will deliver us from our enemies.

Canticle of Zacharias
Luke 1:68-79

Blessed be the Lord ✠ God of Israel; * because he hath visited and wrought the redemption of his people:

And hath raised up an horn of salvation to us, * in the house of David his servant:

As he spoke by the mouth of his holy Prophets, * who are from the beginning:

Salvation from our enemies, * and from the hand of all that hate us:

To perform mercy to our fathers, * and to remember his holy testament,

The oath, which he swore to Abraham our father, * that he would grant to us,

That being delivered from the hand of our enemies, * we may serve him without fear,

In holiness and justice before him, * all our days.

And thou, child, shalt be called the prophet of the Highest: * for thou shalt go before the face of the Lord to prepare his ways:

Thursday - Lauds

Ad dandam sciéntiam salútis plebi eius: * in remissiónem peccatórum eórum:

Per víscera misericórdiæ Dei nostri: * in quibus visitávit nos, óriens ex alto:

Illumináre his, qui in ténebris, et in umbra mortis sedent: * ad dirigéndos pedes nostros in viam pacis.

Ant. In sanctitáte serviámus Dómino, et liberábit nos ab inimícis nostris.

Kýrie, eléison. Christe, eléison. Kýrie, eléison.

Pater noster, qui es in cælis, sanctificétur nomen tuum: advéniat regnum tuum: fiat volúntas tua, sicut in cælo et in terra. Panem nostrum cotidiánum da nobis hódie: et dimítte nobis débita nostra, sicut et nos dimíttimus debitóribus nostris:

℣. Et ne nos indúcas in tentatiónem:

℟. Sed líbera nos a malo.

℣. Dóminus vobíscum.

℟. Et cum spíritu tuo.

℣. Benedicámus Dómino.

℟. Deo grátias.

℣. Fidélium ánimæ per misericórdiam Dei requiéscant in pace.

℟. Amen.

℣. Divínum auxílium máneat semper nobíscum.

℟. Et cum frátribus nostris abséntibus. Amen.

To give knowledge of salvation to his people, * unto the remission of their sins:

Through the bowels of the mercy of our God, * in which the Orient from on high hath visited us:

To enlighten them that sit in darkness, and in the shadow of death: * to direct our feet into the way of peace.

Ant. In holiness let us serve the Lord, and he will deliver us from our enemies.

Lord have mercy upon us, Christ have mercy upon us, Lord have mercy upon us

Our Father, who art in heaven, Hallowed be thy name. Thy kingdom come. Thy will be done on earth as it is in heaven. Give us this day our daily bread. And forgive us our trespasses, as we forgive those who trespass against us.

℣. And lead us not into temptation:

℟. But deliver us from evil.

℣. The Lord be with you.

℟. And with your spirit.

℣. Let us bless the Lord.

℟. Thanks be to God.

℣. May the souls of the faithful, through the mercy of God, rest in peace.

℟. Amen.

℣. May the divine assistance remain with us always.

℟. And with our brothers, who are absent. Amen.

FRIDAY - LAUDS

℣. Deus in adiutórium meum inténde.

℟. Dómine, ad adiuvándum me festína. Glória Patri, et Fílio, * et Spirítui Sancto. Sicut erat in princípio, et nunc, et semper, * et in sǽcula sæculórum. Amen. Allelúia.

Psalmus 66

DEUS misereátur nostri, et benedícat nobis: * illúminet vultum suum super nos, et misereátur nostri.

Ut cognoscámus in terra viam tuam, * in ómnibus géntibus salutáre tuum.

Confiteántur tibi pópuli, Deus: * confiteántur tibi pópuli omnes.

Læt, et exsúltent gentes: † quóniam iúdicas pópulos in æquitáte, * et gentes in terra dírigis.

Confiteántur tibi pópuli, Deus, † confiteántur tibi pópuli omnes: * terra dedit fructum suum.

Benedícat nos Deus, Deus noster, benedícat nos Deus: * et métuant eum omnes fines terræ.

Glória Patri, et Fílio, * et Spirítui Sancto.

℣. O God, come to my assistance;

℟. O Lord, make haste to help me. Glory be to the Father, and to the Son, * and to the Holy Ghost. As it was in the beginning, is now, * and ever shall be, world without end. Amen. Alleluia.

Psalm 66

MAY God have mercy on us, and bless us: * may he cause the light of his countenance to shine upon us, and may he have mercy on us.

That we may know thy way upon earth: * thy salvation in all nations.

Let people confess to thee, O God: * let all people give praise to thee.

Let the nations be glad and rejoice: † for thou judgest the people with justice, * and directest the nations upon earth.

Let the people, O God, confess to thee: † let all the people give praise to thee: * the earth hath yielded her fruit.

May God, our God bless us, may God bless us: * and all the ends of the earth fear him.

Glory be to the Father, and to the Son, * and to the Holy Ghost.

Friday - Lauds

Sicut erat in princípio, et nunc, et semper, * et in sǽcula sæculórum. Amen.

Per annum, Ant. Spíritu principáli † confírma cor meum, Deus.

Tempore paschali, Ant. Allelúia, † allelúia, allelúia.

Et dicitur tres psalmi sequentes sub una antiphona.

Psalmus 50 [1]

MISERÉRE mei, Deus, * secúndum magnam misericórdiam tuam.

Et secúndum multitúdinem miseratiónum tuárum, * dele iniquitátem meam.

Amplius lava me ab iniquitáte mea: * et a peccáto meo munda me.

Quóniam iniquitátem meam ego cognósco: * et peccátum meum contra me est semper.

Tibi soli peccávi, et malum coram te feci: * ut iustificéris in sermónibus tuis, et vincas cum iudicáris.

Ecce enim, in iniquitátibus concéptus sum: * et in peccátis concépit me mater mea.

Ecce enim, veritátem dilexísti: * incérta et occúlta sapiéntiæ tuæ manifestásti mihi.

Aspérges me hyssópo, et mundábor: * lavábis me, et super nivem dealbábor.

Audítui meo dabis gáudium et lætítiam: * et exsultábunt ossa humiliáta.

As it was in the beginning, is now, * and ever shall be, world without end. Amen.

During the year, Ant. With a perfect spirit † strengthen my heart, O God.

Paschaltide, Ant. Alleluia, † alleluia, alleluia.

And the three following psalms are said under this one antiphon.

Psalm 50 [1]

HAVE mercy on me, O God, * according to thy great mercy.

And according to the multitude of thy tender mercies * blot out my iniquity.

Wash me yet more from my iniquity, * and cleanse me from my sin.

For I know my iniquity, * and my sin is always before me.

To thee only have I sinned, and have done evil before thee: * that thou mayst be justified in thy words, and mayst overcome when thou art judged.

For behold I was conceived in iniquities; * and in sins did my mother conceive me.

For behold thou hast loved truth: * the uncertain and hidden things of thy wisdom thou hast made manifest to me.

Thou shalt sprinkle me with hyssop, and I shall be cleansed: * thou shalt wash me, and I shall be made whiter than snow.

To my hearing thou shalt give joy and gladness: * and the bones

Friday - Lauds

Avérte fáciem tuam a peccátis meis: * et omnes iniquitátes meas dele.

Cor mundum crea in me, Deus: * et spíritum rectum ínnova in viscéribus meis.

Ne proícias me a fácie tua: * et spíritum sanctum tuum ne áuferas a me.

Redde mihi lætítiam salutáris tui: * et spíritu principáli confírma me.

Docébo iníquos vias tuas: * et ímpii ad te converténtur.

Líbera me de sanguínibus, Deus, Deus salútis meæ: * et exsultábit lingua mea iustítiam tuam.

Dómine, lábia mea apéries: * et os meum annuntiábit laudem tuam.

Quóniam si voluísses sacrifícium, dedíssem útique: * holocáustis non delectáberis.

Sacrifícium Deo spíritus contribulátus: * cor contrítum, et humiliátum, Deus, non despícies.

Benígne fac, Dómine, in bona voluntáte tua Sion: * ut ædificéntur muri Ierúsalem.

Tunc acceptábis sacrifícium iustítiæ, oblatiónes, et holocáusta: * tunc impónent super altáre tuum vítulos.

that have been humbled shall rejoice.

Turn away thy face from my sins, * and blot out all my iniquities.

Create a clean heart in me, O God: * and renew a right spirit within my bowels.

Cast me not away from thy face; * and take not thy holy spirit from me.

Restore unto me the joy of thy salvation, * and strengthen me with a perfect spirit.

I will teach the unjust thy ways: * and the wicked shall be converted to thee.

Deliver me from blood, O God, thou God of my salvation: * and my tongue shall extol thy justice.

O Lord, thou wilt open my lips: * and my mouth shall declare thy praise.

For if thou hadst desired sacrifice, I would indeed have given it: * with burnt offerings thou wilt not be delighted.

A sacrifice to God is an afflicted spirit: * a contrite and humbled heart, O God, thou wilt not despise.

Deal favourably, O Lord, in thy good will with Sion; * that the walls of Jerusalem may be built up.

Then shalt thou accept the sacrifice of justice, oblations and whole burnt offerings: * then shall they lay calves upon thy altar.

Ant. Spíritu principáli confírma cor meum, Deus.

Ant. In Israël † magnum nomen eius.

Psalmus 75 [2]

Notus in Iudǽa Deus: * in Israël magnum nomen eius.

Et factus est in pace locus eius: * et habitátio eius in Sion.

Ibi confrégit poténtias árcuum, * scutum, gládium, et bellum.

Illúminans tu mirabíliter a móntibus ætérnis: * turbáti sunt omnes insipiéntes corde.

Dormiérunt somnum suum: * et nihil invenérunt omnes viri divitiárum in mánibus suis.

Ab increpatióne tua, Deus Iacob, * dormitavérunt qui ascendérunt equos.

Tu terríbilis es, et quis resístet tibi? * ex tunc ira tua.

De cælo audítum fecísti iudícium: * terra trémuit et quiévit,

Cum exsúrgeret in iudícium Deus, * ut salvos fáceret omnes mansuétos terræ.

Quóniam cogitátio hóminis confitébitur tibi: * et relíquiæ cogitatiónis diem festum agent tibi.

Vovéte, et réddite Dómino, Deo vestro: * omnes, qui in circúitu eius affértis múnera.

Terríbili et ei qui aufert spíritum príncipum, * terríbili apud reges terræ.

Ant. With a perfect spirit strengthen my heart, O God.

Ant. In Israel † His name is great.

Psalm 75 [2]

In Judea God is known: * his name is great in Israel.

And his place is in peace: * and his abode in Sion:

There hath he broken the powers of bows, * the shield, the sword, and the battle.

Thou enlightenest wonderfully from the everlasting hills. * All the foolish of heart were troubled.

They have slept their sleep; * and all the men of riches have found nothing in their hands.

At thy rebuke, O God of Jacob, * they have all slumbered that mounted on horseback.

Thou art terrible, and who shall resist thee? * from that time thy wrath.

Thou hast caused judgment to be heard from heaven: * the earth trembled and was still,

When God arose in judgment, * to save all the meek of the earth.

For the thought of man shall give praise to thee: * and the remainders of the thought shall keep holiday to thee.

Vow ye, and pay to the Lord your God: * all you that are round about him bring presents.

To him that is terrible, even to him who taketh away the spirit of princes: * to the terrible with the kings of the earth.

Friday - Lauds 81

Ant. In Israël magnum nomen eius.

Ant. Bonum est † confitéri Dómino.

Et non repetitur in psalmo.

Psalmus 91 [3]

Bonum est confitéri Dómino: * et psállere nómini tuo, Altíssime.

Ad annuntiándum mane misericórdiam tuam: * et veritátem tuam per noctem.

In decachórdo, psaltério: * cum cántico, in cíthara.

Quia delectásti me, Dómine, in factúra tua: * et in opéribus mánuum tuárum exsultábo.

Quam magnificáta sunt ópera tua, Dómine! * nimis profúndæ factæ sunt cogitatiónes tuæ.

Vir insípiens non cognóscet: * et stultus non intélleget hæc.

Cum exórti fúerint peccatóres sicut fænum: * et apparúerint omnes, qui operántur iniquitátem:

Ut intéreant in sǽculum sǽculi: * tu autem Altíssimus in ætérnum, Dómine.

Quóniam ecce inimíci tui, Dómine, quóniam ecce inimíci tui períbunt: * et dispergéntur omnes, qui operántur iniquitátem.

Et exaltábitur sicut unicórnis cornu meum: * et senéctus mea in misericórdia úberi.

Et despéxit óculus meus inimícos meos: * et in insurgéntibus

Ant. In Israel His name is great.

Ant. It is a good thing † to give thanks unto the Lord.

It is not repeated in the psalm.

Psalm 91 [3]

It is good to give praise to the Lord: * and to sing to thy name, O most High.

To shew forth thy mercy in the morning, * and thy truth in the night:

Upon an instrument of ten strings, upon the psaltery: * with a canticle upon the harp.

For thou hast given me, O Lord, a delight in thy doings: * and in the works of thy hands I shall rejoice.

O Lord, how great are thy works! * thy thoughts are exceeding deep.

The senseless man shall not know: * nor will the fool understand these things.

When the wicked shall spring up as grass: * and all the workers of iniquity shall appear:

That they may perish for ever and ever: * but thou, O Lord, art most high for evermore.

For behold thy enemies, O Lord, for behold thy enemies shall perish: * and all the workers of iniquity shall be scattered.

But my horn shall be exalted like that of the unicorn: * and my old age in plentiful mercy.

My eye also hath looked down upon my enemies: * and my ear

82 Friday - Lauds

in me malignántibus áudiet auris mea.

Iustus, ut palma florébit: * sicut cedrus Líbani multiplicábitur.

Plantáti in domo Dómini, * in átriis domus Dei nostri florébunt.

Adhuc multiplicabúntur in senécta úberi: * et bene patiéntes erunt, ut annúntient:

Quóniam rectus Dóminus, Deus noster: * et non est iníquitas in eo.

Per annum, Ant. Bonum est confitéri Dómino.

Tempore paschali, Ant. Allelúia, allelúia, allelúia.

Canticum Feriale

Ant. Dómine, † audívi audítum tuum, et tímui. (*T.P.* Allelúia.)

Et non repetitur in cantico.

Canticum Habacuc [4]
Hab. 3:2-19

DÓMINE, audívi auditiónem tuam, * et tímui.

Dómine, opus tuum, * in médio annórum vivífica illud;

In medio annórum notum fácies: * cum irátus fúeris, misericórdiæ recordáberis.

Deus ab Austro véniet, * et Sanctus de monte Pharan:

shall hear of the downfall of the malignant that rise up against me.

The just shall flourish like the palm tree: * he shall grow up like the cedar of Libanus.

They that are planted in the house of the Lord * shall flourish in the courts of the house of our God.

They shall still increase in a fruitful old age: * and shall be well treated, that they may shew,

That the Lord our God is righteous, * and there is no iniquity in him.

During the year, Ant. It is a good thing to give thanks unto the Lord.

Paschaltide, Ant. Alleluia, alleluia, alleluia.

Ferial Canticle

Ant. O Lord, † I heard Thy message, and I was afraid. (*P.T.* Alleluia.)

It is not repeated in the canticle.

Canticle of Habacuc [4]
Hab. 3:2-19

O Lord, I have heard thy hearing, * and was afraid.

O Lord, thy work, * in the midst of the years bring it to life:

In the midst of the years thou shalt make it known: * when thou art angry, thou wilt remember mercy.

God will come from the south, * and the holy one from mount Pharan:

Friday - Lauds

Opéruit cælos glória eius, * et laudis eius plena est terra.

Splendor eius ut lux erit, * córnua in mánibus eius: Ibi abscóndita est fortitúdo eius. * Ante fáciem eius ibit mors: Et egrediétur diábolus ante pedes eius. * Stetit, et mensus est terram; Aspéxit, et dissólvit Gentes, * et contríti sunt montes sǽculi:

Incurváti sunt colles mundi * ab itinéribus æternitátis eius.

Pro iniquitáte vidi tentória Æthiópiæ; * turbabúntur pelles terræ Mádian.

Numquid in flumínibus irátus es, Dómine? † aut in flumínibus furor tuus? * vel in mari indignátio tua?

Qui ascéndes super equos tuos, * et quadrígæ tuæ salvátio.

Súscitans suscitábis arcum tuum, * iuraménta tríbubus quæ locútus es;

Flúvios scindes terræ. † Vidérunt te, et doluérunt montes; * gurges aquárum tránsiit:

Dedit abýssus vocem suam; * altitúdo manus suas levávit.

Sol et luna stetérunt in habitáculo suo: † in luce sagittárum tuárum, * ibunt in splendóre fulgurántis hastæ tuæ.

His glory covered the heavens, * and the earth is full of his praise.

His brightness shall be as the light; * horns are in his hands: There is his strength hid: * Death shall go before his face.

And the devil shall go forth before his feet. * He stood and measured the earth.

He beheld, and melted the nations: * and the ancient mountains were crushed to pieces.

The hills of the world were bowed down * by the journeys of his eternity.

I saw the tents of Ethiopia for their iniquity, * the curtains of the land of Madian shall be troubled.

Wast thou angry, O Lord, with the rivers? † or was thy wrath upon the rivers? * or thy indignation in the sea?

Who will ride upon thy horses: * and thy chariots are salvation.

Thou wilt surely take up thy bow: * according to the oaths which thou hast spoken to the tribes.

Thou wilt divide the rivers of the earth. † The mountains saw thee, and were grieved: * the great body of waters passed away.

The deep put forth its voice: * the deep lifted up its hands.

The sun and the moon stood still in their habitation, † in the light of thy arrows, * they shall go in the brightness of thy glittering spear.

84 Friday - Lauds

In frémitu conculcábis terram; * in furóre obstupefácies gentes.

Egréssus es in salútem pópuli tui, * in salútem cum Christo tuo:

Percussísti caput de domo ímpii, * denudásti fundaméntum eius usque ad collum.

Maledixísti sceptris eius, † cápiti bellatórum eius, * veniéntibus ut turbo ad dispergéndum me:

Exsultátio eórum, * sicut eius qui dévorat páuperem in abscóndito.

Viam fecísti in mari equis tuis, * in luto aquárum multárum.

Audívi, et conturbátus est venter meus; * a voce contremuérunt lábia mea.

Ingrediátur putrédo in óssibus meis, * et subter me scáteat:

Ut requiéscam in die tribulatiónis, * ut ascéndam ad pópulum accínctum nostrum.

Ficus enim non florébit, * et non erit germen in víneis;

Mentiétur opus olívæ, * et arva non áfferent cibum:

Abscindétur de óvili pecus, * et non erit arméntum in præsépibus.

Ego autem in Dómino gaudébo; * et exsultábo in Deo Iesu meo.

In thy anger thou wilt tread the earth under foot: * in thy wrath thou wilt astonish the nations.

Thou wentest forth for the salvation of thy people: * for salvation with thy Christ.

Thou struckest the head of the house of the wicked: * thou hast laid bare his foundation even to the neck.

Thou hast cursed his sceptres, † the head of his warriors, * them that came out as a whirlwind to scatter me.

Their joy * was like that of him that devoureth the poor man in secret.

Thou madest a way in the sea for thy horses, * in the mud of many waters.

I have heard and my bowels were troubled: * my lips trembled at the voice.

Let rottenness enter into my bones, * and swarm under me.

That I may rest in the day of tribulation: * that I may go up to our people that are girded.

For the fig tree shall not blossom: * and there shall be no spring in the vines.

The labour of the olive tree shall fail: * and the fields shall yield no food:

The flock shall be cut off from the fold, * and there shall be no herd in the stalls.

But I will rejoice in the Lord: * and I will joy in God my Jesus.

Friday - Lauds

Deus Dóminus fortitúdo mea, * et ponet pedes meos quasi cervórum:

Et super excélsa mea dedúcet me victor * in psalmis canéntem.

Ant. Dómine, audívi audítum tuum, et tímui. (*T.P.* Allelúia.)

Canticum Festivum

Ant. In Dómino iustificábitur † et laudábitur omne semen Israël. (*T.P.* Allelúia.)

Canticum Isaiæ [4]

Isa. 45:15-26

VERE tu es Deus abscónditus, * Deus Israël, Salvátor.

Confúsi sunt, et erubuérunt omnes: * simul abiérunt in confusiónem fabricatóres errórum.

Israël salvátus est in Dómino salúte ætérna: * non confundémini, et non erubescétis usque in sǽculum sǽculi.

Quia hæc dicit Dóminus creans cælos, † ipse Deus formans terram, et fáciens eam, * ipse plastes eius:

Non in vanum creávit eam, † ut habitarétur, formávit eam: * Ego Dóminus, et non est álius.

Non in abscóndito locútus sum, * in loco terræ tenebróso:

Non dixi sémini Iacob frustra: Quǽrite me: * ego Dóminus loquens iustítiam, annúntians recta.

The Lord God is my strength: * and he will make my feet like the feet of harts:

And he the conqueror will lead me upon my high places * singing psalms.

Ant. O Lord, I heard Thy message, and I was afraid. (*P.T.* Alleluia.)

Festal Canticle

Ant. In the Lord † shall all the seed of Israel be justified and blessed. (*P.T.* Alleluia.)

Canticle of Isaias [4]

Is. 45:15-26

VERILY thou art a hidden God, * the God of Israel the saviour.

They are all confounded and ashamed: * the forgers of errors are gone together into confusion.

Israel is saved in the Lord with an eternal salvation: * you shall not be confounded, and you shall not be ashamed for ever and ever.

For thus saith the Lord that created the heavens, † God himself that formed the earth, and made it, * the very maker thereof:

He did not create it in vain: † he formed it to be inhabited. * I am the Lord, and there is no other.

I have not spoken in secret, * in a dark place of the earth:

I have not said to the seed of Jacob: Seek me in vain. * I am the Lord that speak justice, that declare right things.

86 Friday - Lauds

Congregámini, et veníte, et accédite simul * qui salváti estis ex géntibus:

Nesciérunt qui levant lignum sculptúræ suæ, * et rogant deum non salvántem.

Annuntiáte, et veníte, et consiliámini simul: * Quis audítum fecit hoc ab inítio, ex tunc prædíxit illud?

Numquid non ego Dóminus, † et non est ultra Deus absque me? * Deus iustus, et salvans non est præter me.

Convertímini ad me, et salvi éritis, omnes fines terræ: * quia ego Deus, et non est álius.

In memetípso iurávi, † egrediétur de ore meo iustítiæ verbum, * et non revertétur:

Quia mihi curvábitur omne genu, * et iurábit omnis lingua.

Ergo in Dómino, dicet, meæ sunt iustítiæ et impérium: * ad eum vénient, et confundéntur omnes qui repúgnant ei.

In Dómino iustificábitur, et laudábitur * omne semen Israël.

Ant. In Dómino iustificábitur et laudábitur omne semen Israël. (*T.P.* Allelúia.)

———

Ant. In tympano et choro, † in cordis et órgano laudáte Deum.

Assemble yourselves, and come, and draw near together, * ye that are saved of the Gentiles:

They have no knowledge that set up the wood of their graven work, * and pray to a god that cannot save.

Tell ye, and come, and consult together: * who hath declared this from the beginning, who hath foretold this from that time?

Have not I the Lord, † and there is no God else besides me? * A just God and a saviour, there is none besides me.

Be converted to me, and you shall be saved, all ye ends of the earth: * for I am God, and there is no other.

I have sworn by myself, † the word of justice shall go out of my mouth, * and shall not return:

For every knee shall be bowed to me, * and every tongue shall swear.

Therefore shall he say: In the Lord are my justices and empire: * they shall come to him, and all that resist him shall be confounded.

In the Lord shall all the seed * of Israel be justified and praised.

Ant. In the Lord shall all the seed of Israel be justified and blessed. (*P.T.* Alleluia.)

———

Ant. Praise him with timbrel and dance: † praise him with strings and flute.

Friday - Lauds

Tempore paschali, Ant. Allelúia, † allelúia, allelúia.

Psalmus 148 [5]

Laudáte Dóminum de cælis: * laudáte eum in excélsis.

Laudáte eum, omnes Angeli eius: * laudáte eum, omnes virtútes eius.
Laudáte eum, sol et luna: * laudáte eum, omnes stellæ et lumen.
Laudáte eum, cæli cælórum: * et aquæ omnes, quæ super cælos sunt, laudent nomen Dómini.

Quia ipse dixit, et facta sunt: * ipse mandávit, et creáta sunt.

Státuit ea in ætérnum, et in sǽculum sǽculi: * præcéptum pósuit, et non præteríbit.

Laudáte Dóminum de terra, * dracónes, et omnes abýssi.
Ignis, grando, nix, glácies, spíritus procellárum: * quæ fáciunt verbum eius:
Montes, et omnes colles: * ligna fructífera, et omnes cedri.
Béstiæ, et univérsa pécora: * serpéntes, et vólucres pennátæ:
Reges terræ, et omnes pópuli: * príncipes, et omnes iúdices terræ.

Iúvenes, et vírgines: † senes cum iunióribus laudent nomen Dómini: * quia exaltátum est nomen eius solíus.

Paschaltide, Ant. Alleluia, † alleluia, alleluia.

Psalm 148 [5]

Praise ye the Lord from the heavens * praise ye him in the high places.
Praise ye him, all his angels: * praise ye him, all his hosts.

Praise ye him, O sun and moon: * praise him, all ye stars and light.

Praise him, ye heavens of heavens: * and let all the waters that are above the heavens, praise the name of the Lord.
For he spoke, and they were made: * he commanded, and they were created.
He hath established them for ever, and for ages of ages: * he hath made a decree, and it shall not pass away.
Praise the Lord from the earth, * ye dragons, and all ye deeps:
Fire, hail, snow, ice, stormy winds * which fulfill his word:

Mountains and all hills, * fruitful trees and all cedars:
Beasts and all cattle: * serpents and feathered fowls:
Kings of the earth and all people: * princes and all judges of the earth:
Young men and maidens: † let the old with the younger, praise the name of the Lord: * For his name alone is exalted.

88 Friday - Lauds

Conféssio eius super cælum et terram: * et exaltávit cornu pópuli sui.
Hymnus ómnibus sanctis eius: * fíliis Israël, pópulo appropinquánti sibi.
Hic non dicitur Gloria Patri.

Psalmus 149 [6]

CANTÁTE Dómino cánticum novum: * laus eius in ecclésia sanctórum.

Lætétur Israël in eo, qui fecit eum: * et fílii Sion exsúltent in rege suo.

Laudent nomen eius in choro: * in týmpano, et psaltério psallant ei:

Quia beneplácitum est Dómino in pópulo suo: * et exaltábit mansuétos in salútem.

Exsultábunt sancti in glória: * lætabúntur in cubílibus suis.

Exaltatiónes Dei in gútture eórum: * et gládii ancípites in mánibus eórum.

Ad faciéndam vindíctam in natiónibus: * increpatiónes in pópulis.

Ad alligándos reges eórum in compédibus: * et nóbiles eórum in mánicis férreis.

Ut fáciant in eis iudícium conscríptum: * glória hæc est ómnibus sanctis eius.

Hic non dicitur Gloria Patri.

The praise of him is above heaven and earth: * and he hath exalted the horn of his people.
A hymn to all his saints: to the children of Israel, a people approaching him.
Here the Glory be is not said.

Psalm 149 [6]

SING ye to the Lord a new canticle: * let his praise be in the church of the saints.

Let Israel rejoice in him that made him: * and let the children of Sion be joyful in their king.

Let them praise his name in choir: * let them sing to him with the timbrel and the psaltery.

For the Lord is well pleased with his people: * and he will exalt the meek unto salvation.

The saints shall rejoice in glory: * they shall be joyful in their beds.

The high praises of God shall be in their mouth: * and twoedged swords in their hands:

To execute vengeance upon the nations, * chastisements among the people:

To bind their kings with fetters, * and their nobles with manacles of iron.

To execute upon them the judgment that is written: * this glory is to all his saints.

Here the Glory be is not said.

Friday - Lauds

Psalmus 150 [7]

Laudáte Dóminum in sanctis eius: * laudáte eum in firmaménto virtútis eius.

Laudáte eum in virtútibus eius: * laudáte eum secúndum multitúdinem magnitúdinis eius.

Laudáte eum in sono tubæ: * laudáte eum in psaltério, et cíthara.

Laudáte eum in týmpano, et choro: * laudáte eum in chordis, et órgano.

Laudáte eum in cýmbalis benesonántibus: † laudáte eum in cýmbalis iubilatiónis: * omnis spíritus laudet Dóminum.

Glória Patri, et Fílio, * et Spirítui Sancto.

Sicut erat in princípio, et nunc, et semper, * et in sǽcula sæculórum. Amen.

Ant. In tympano et choro, in cordis et órgano laudáte Deum.

Tempore paschali, Ant. Allelúia, allelúia, allelúia.

Capitulum   Rom. 13:12-13

Nox præcéssit, dies autem appropinquávit. † Abiciámus ergo ópera tenebrárum, et induámur arma lucis. * Sicut in die honéste ambulémus.

℞. Deo grátias.

℞.*br.* Sana ánimam meam, * quia peccávi tibi.

℞. Sana ánimam meam, * quia peccávi tibi.

Psalm 150 [7]

Praise ye the Lord in his holy places: * praise ye him in the firmament of his power.

Praise ye him for his mighty acts: * praise ye him according to the multitude of his greatness.

Praise him with sound of trumpet: * praise him with psaltery and harp.

Praise him with timbrel and choir: * praise him with strings and organs.

Praise him on high sounding cymbals: † praise him on cymbals of joy: * let every spirit praise the Lord.

Glory be to the Father, and to the Son, * and to the Holy Ghost.

As it was in the beginning, is now, * and ever shall be, world without end. Amen.

Ant. Praise him with timbrel and dance: praise him with strings and flute.

Paschaltide, Ant. Alleluia, alleluia, alleluia.

Chapter   Rom. 13:12-13

The night is passed, and the day is at hand. Let us therefore cast off the works of darkness, and put on the armour of light. Let us walk honestly, as in the day.

℞. Thanks be to God.

℞.*br.* Heal my soul, * for I have sinned against thee.

℞. Heal my soul, * for I have sinned against thee.

℣. Ego dixi: Dómine, miserére mei

℟. Quia peccávi tibi.

℣. Glória Patri, et Fílio, * et Spirítui Sancto.

℟. Sana ánimam meam, * quia peccávi tibi.

Hymnus

Ætérna cæli glória,
Beáta spes mortálium,
Celsi Tonántis Unice,
Castǽque proles Vírginis:

Da déxteram surgéntibus,
Exsúrgat et mens sóbria,
Flagrans et in laudem Dei
Grates repéndat débitas.

Ortus refúlget Lúcifer,
Sparsámque lucem núntiat:
Cadit calígo nóctium:
Lux sancta nos illúminet.

Manénsque nostris sénsibus,
Noctem repéllat sǽculi,
Omníque fine diéi
Purgáta servet péctora.

Quæsíta iam primum fides
Radícet altis sénsibus:
Secúnda spes congáudeat,
Qua maior exstat cáritas.

Deo Patri sit glória,
Eiúsque soli Fílio,
Cum Spíritu Paráclito,

℣. I said: O Lord, be thou merciful to me

℟. For I have sinned against thee.

℣. Glory be to the Father, and to the Son, * and to the Holy Ghost.

℟. Heal my soul, * for I have sinned against thee.

Hymn

O Christ, whose glory fills the heaven,
Our only hope, in mercy given;
Child of a Virgin meek and pure;
Son of the Highest evermore:

Grant us thine aid thy praise to sing,
As opening days new duties bring;
That with the light our life may be
Renewed and sanctified by thee.

The morning star fades from the sky,
The sun breaks forth; night's shadows fly:
O Thou, true Light, upon us shine:
Our darkness turn to light divine.

Within us grant thy light to dwell;
And from our souls dark sins expel;
Cleanse thou our minds from stain of ill,
And with thy peace our bosoms fill.

To us strong faith forever give,
With joyous hope, in thee to live;
That life's rough way may ever be
Made strong and pure by charity.

All laud to God the Father be;
All praise, Eternal Son, to thee;
All glory, as is ever meet,

Friday - Lauds

Et nunc et in perpétuum.
Amen.

℣. Repléti sumus mane misericórdia tua.

℞. Exsultávimus, et delectáti sumus.

Ant. Per víscera misericórdiæ † Dei nostri visitávit nos Oriens ex alto.

Canticum Zachariæ
Luc. 1:68-79

BENEDÍCTUS ✠ Dóminus, Deus Israël: * quia visitávit, et fecit redemptiónem plebis suæ:

Et eréxit cornu salútis nobis: * in domo David, púeri sui.

Sicut locútus est per os sanctórum, * qui a sǽculo sunt, prophetárum eius:

Salútem ex inimícis nostris, * et de manu ómnium, qui odérunt nos.

Ad faciéndam misericórdiam cum pátribus nostris: * et memorári testaménti sui sancti.

Iusiurándum, quod iurávit ad Abraham patrem nostrum, * datúrum se nobis:

Ut sine timóre, de manu inimicórum nostrórum liberáti, * serviámus illi.

In sanctitáte, et iustítia coram ipso, * ómnibus diébus nostris.

Et tu, puer, Prophéta Altíssimi vocáberis: * præíbis enim ante fáciem Dómini, paráre vias eius:

To God the Holy Paraclete.
Amen.

℣. We are filled in the morning with thy mercy.

℞. And we have rejoiced, and are delighted.

Ant. Through the tender mercy † of our God, the dayspring from on high has visited us.

Canticle of Zacharias
Luke 1:68-79

Blessed be the Lord ✠ God of Israel; * because he hath visited and wrought the redemption of his people:

And hath raised up an horn of salvation to us, * in the house of David his servant:

As he spoke by the mouth of his holy Prophets, * who are from the beginning:

Salvation from our enemies, * and from the hand of all that hate us:

To perform mercy to our fathers, * and to remember his holy testament,

The oath, which he swore to Abraham our father, * that he would grant to us,

That being delivered from the hand of our enemies, * we may serve him without fear,

In holiness and justice before him, * all our days.

And thou, child, shalt be called the prophet of the Highest: * for thou shalt go before the face of the Lord to prepare his ways:

Friday - Lauds

Ad dandam sciéntiam salútis plebi eius: * in remissiónem peccatórum eórum:

Per víscera misericórdiæ Dei nostri: * in quibus visitávit nos, óriens ex alto:

Illumináre his, qui in ténebris, et in umbra mortis sedent: * ad dirigéndos pedes nostros in viam pacis.

Ant. Per víscera misericórdiæ Dei nostri visitávit nos Oriens ex alto.

Kýrie, eléison. Christe, eléison. Kýrie, eléison.

Pater noster, qui es in cælis, sanctificétur nomen tuum: advéniat regnum tuum: fiat volúntas tua, sicut in cælo et in terra. Panem nostrum cotidiánum da nobis hódie: et dimítte nobis débita nostra, sicut et nos dimíttimus debitóribus nostris:

℣. Et ne nos indúcas in tentatiónem:

℟. Sed líbera nos a malo.

℣. Dóminus vobíscum.

℟. Et cum spíritu tuo.

℣. Benedicámus Dómino.

℟. Deo grátias.

℣. Fidélium ánimæ per misericórdiam Dei requiéscant in pace.

℟. Amen.

℣. Divínum auxílium máneat semper nobíscum.

℟. Et cum frátribus nostris abséntibus. Amen.

To give knowledge of salvation to his people, * unto the remission of their sins:

Through the bowels of the mercy of our God, * in which the Orient from on high hath visited us:

To enlighten them that sit in darkness, and in the shadow of death: * to direct our feet into the way of peace.

Ant. Through the tender mercy of our God, the dayspring from on high has visited us.

Lord have mercy upon us, Christ have mercy upon us, Lord have mercy upon us

Our Father, who art in heaven, Hallowed be thy name. Thy kingdom come. Thy will be done on earth as it is in heaven. Give us this day our daily bread. And forgive us our trespasses, as we forgive those who trespass against us.

℣. And lead us not into temptation:

℟. But deliver us from evil.

℣. The Lord be with you.

℟. And with your spirit.

℣. Let us bless the Lord.

℟. Thanks be to God.

℣. May the souls of the faithful, through the mercy of God, rest in peace.

℟. Amen.

℣. May the divine assistance remain with us always.

℟. And with our brothers, who are absent. Amen.

SATURDAY - LAUDS

℣. Deus in adiutórium meum inténde.

℟. Dómine, ad adiuvándum me festína. Glória Patri, et Fílio, * et Spirítui Sancto. Sicut erat in princípio, et nunc, et semper, * et in sǽcula sæculórum. Amen. Allelúia.

Psalmus 66

DEUS misereátur nostri, et benedícat nobis: * illúminet vultum suum super nos, et misereátur nostri.

Ut cognoscámus in terra viam tuam, * in ómnibus géntibus salutáre tuum.

Confiteántur tibi pópuli, Deus: * confiteántur tibi pópuli omnes.

Lætténtur et exsúltent gentes: † quóniam iúdicas pópulos in æquitáte, * et gentes in terra dírigis.

Confiteántur tibi pópuli, Deus, † confiteántur tibi pópuli omnes: * terra dedit fructum suum.

Benedícat nos Deus, Deus noster, benedícat nos Deus: * et métuant eum omnes fines terræ.

Glória Patri, et Fílio, * et Spirítui Sancto.

℣. O God, come to my assistance;

℟. O Lord, make haste to help me. Glory be to the Father, and to the Son, * and to the Holy Ghost. As it was in the beginning, is now, * and ever shall be, world without end. Amen. Alleluia.

Psalm 66

MAY God have mercy on us, and bless us: * may he cause the light of his countenance to shine upon us, and may he have mercy on us.

That we may know thy way upon earth: * thy salvation in all nations.

Let people confess to thee, O God: * let all people give praise to thee.

Let the nations be glad and rejoice: † for thou judgest the people with justice, * and directest the nations upon earth.

Let the people, O God, confess to thee: † let all the people give praise to thee: * the earth hath yielded her fruit.

May God, our God bless us, may God bless us: * and all the ends of the earth fear him.

Glory be to the Father, and to the Son, * and to the Holy Ghost.

Saturday - Lauds

Sicut erat in princípio, et nunc, et semper, * et in sǽcula sæculórum. Amen.

Per annum, Ant. Benígne fac †
in bona voluntáte tua, Dómine.

Tempore paschali, Ant. Allelúia, † allelúia, allelúia.

Et dicitur tres psalmi sequentes sub una antiphona.

Psalmus 50 [1]

MISERÉRE mei, Deus, * secúndum magnam misericórdiam tuam.

Et secúndum multitúdinem miseratiónum tuárum, * dele iniquitátem meam.

Amplius lava me ab iniquitáte mea: * et a peccáto meo munda me.

Quóniam iniquitátem meam ego cognósco: * et peccátum meum contra me est semper.

Tibi soli peccávi, et malum coram te feci: * ut iustificéris in sermónibus tuis, et vincas cum iudicáris.

Ecce enim, in iniquitátibus concéptus sum: * et in peccátis concépit me mater mea.

Ecce enim, veritátem dilexísti: * incérta et occúlta sapiéntiæ tuæ manifestásti mihi.

Aspérges me hyssópo, et mundábor: * lavábis me, et super nivem dealbábor.

Audítui meo dabis gáudium et lætítiam: * et exsultábunt ossa humiliáta.

As it was in the beginning, is now, * and ever shall be, world without end. Amen.

During the year, Ant. Deal graciously † O Lord in thy goodness.

Paschaltide, Ant. Alleluia, † alleluia, alleluia.

And the three following psalms are said under this one antiphon.

Psalm 50 [1]

HAVE mercy on me, O God, * according to thy great mercy.

And according to the multitude of thy tender mercies * blot out my iniquity.

Wash me yet more from my iniquity, * and cleanse me from my sin.

For I know my iniquity, * and my sin is always before me.

To thee only have I sinned, and have done evil before thee: * that thou mayst be justified in thy words, and mayst overcome when thou art judged.

For behold I was conceived in iniquities; * and in sins did my mother conceive me.

For behold thou hast loved truth: * the uncertain and hidden things of thy wisdom thou hast made manifest to me.

Thou shalt sprinkle me with hyssop, and I shall be cleansed: * thou shalt wash me, and I shall be made whiter than snow.

To my hearing thou shalt give joy and gladness: * and the bones

Saturday - Lauds

Avérte fáciem tuam a peccátis meis: * et omnes iniquitátes meas dele.

Cor mundum crea in me, Deus: * et spíritum rectum ínnova in viscéribus meis.

Ne proícias me a fácie tua: * et spíritum sanctum tuum ne áuferas a me.

Redde mihi lætítiam salutáris tui: * et spíritu principáli confírma me.

Docébo iníquos vias tuas: * et ímpii ad te converténtur.

Líbera me de sanguínibus, Deus, Deus salútis meæ: * et exsultábit lingua mea iustítiam tuam.

Dómine, lábia mea apéries: * et os meum annuntiábit laudem tuam.

Quóniam si voluísses sacrifícium, dedíssem útique: * holocáustis non delectáberis.

Sacrifícium Deo spíritus contribulátus: * cor contrítum, et humiliátum, Deus, non despícies.

Benígne fac, Dómine, in bona voluntáte tua Sion: * ut ædificéntur muri Ierúsalem.

Tunc acceptábis sacrifícium iustítiæ, oblatiónes, et holocáusta: * tunc impónent super altáre tuum vítulos.

that have been humbled shall rejoice.

Turn away thy face from my sins, * and blot out all my iniquities.

Create a clean heart in me, O God: * and renew a right spirit within my bowels.

Cast me not away from thy face; * and take not thy holy spirit from me.

Restore unto me the joy of thy salvation, * and strengthen me with a perfect spirit.

I will teach the unjust thy ways: * and the wicked shall be converted to thee.

Deliver me from blood, O God, thou God of my salvation: * and my tongue shall extol thy justice.

O Lord, thou wilt open my lips: * and my mouth shall declare thy praise.

For if thou hadst desired sacrifice, I would indeed have given it: * with burnt offerings thou wilt not be delighted.

A sacrifice to God is an afflicted spirit: * a contrite and humbled heart, O God, thou wilt not despise.

Deal favourably, O Lord, in thy good will with Sion; * that the walls of Jerusalem may be built up.

Then shalt thou accept the sacrifice of justice, oblations and whole burnt offerings: * then shall they lay calves upon thy altar.

Ant. Benígne fac in bona voluntáte tua, Dómine.

Ant. In veritáte tua † exáudi me, Dómine.

Si canticum festivum dicitur, Psalmus 142 in duo dividitur. Secus non est divisio.

Psalmus 142 [2]

DÓMINE, exáudi oratiónem meam: † áuribus pércipe obsecratiónem meam in veritáte tua: * exáudi me in tua iustítia.

Et non intres in iudícium cum servo tuo: * quia non iustificábitur in conspéctu tuo omnis vivens.

Quia persecútus est inimícus ánimam meam: * humiliávit in terra vitam meam.

Collocávit me in obscúris sicut mórtuos sǽculi: † et anxiátus est super me spíritus meus, * in me turbátum est cor meum.

Memor fui diérum antiquórum, † meditátus sum in ómnibus opéribus tuis: * in factis mánuum tuárum meditábar.

Expándi manus meas ad te: * ánima mea sicut terra sine aqua tibi.

Velóciter exáudi me, Dómine: * defécit spíritus meus.

Non avértas fáciem tuam a me: * et símilis ero descendéntibus in lacum.

Ant. Deal graciously O Lord in thy goodness.

Ant. In thy truth, † O Lord, listen unto me.

If the festal canticle is said, Psalm 142 is divided in two. Otherwise there is no division.

Psalm 142 [2]

HEAR, O Lord, my prayer: † give ear to my supplication in thy truth: * hear me in thy justice.

And enter not into judgment with thy servant: * for in thy sight no man living shall be justified.

For the enemy hath persecuted my soul: * he hath brought down my life to the earth.

He hath made me to dwell in darkness as those that have been dead of old: † and my spirit is in anguish within me: * my heart within me is troubled.

I remembered the days of old, † I meditated on all thy works: * I meditated upon the works of thy hands.

I stretched forth my hands to thee: * my soul is as earth without water unto thee.

Hear me speedily, O Lord: * my spirit hath fainted away.

Turn not away thy face from me, * lest I be like unto them that go down into the pit.

Divisio [3]

Audítam fac mihi mane misericórdiam tuam: * quia in te sperávi.

Notam fac mihi viam, in qua ámbulem: * quia ad te levávi ánimam meam.

Éripe me de inimícis meis, Dómine, ad te confúgi: * doce me fácere voluntátem tuam, quia Deus meus es tu.

Spíritus tuus bonus dedúcet me in terram rectam: * propter nomen tuum, Dómine, vivificábis me, in æquitáte tua.

Edúces de tribulatióne ánimam meam: * et in misericórdia tua dispérdes inimícos meos.

Et perdes omnes, qui tríbulant ánimam meam: * quóniam ego servus tuus sum.

Per annum, Ant. In veritáte tua exáudi me, Dómine.

Tempore paschali, Ant. Allelúia, allelúia, allelúia.

Canticum Feriale

Ant. Date magnitúdinem † Deo nostro. (*T.P.* Allelúia.)

Canticum Moysi [3]

Deut. 32:1-18

Audíte, cæli, quæ loquor: * áudiat terra verba oris mei.

Concréscat ut plúvia doctrína mea, * fluat ut ros elóquium meum,

Division [3]

Cause me to hear thy mercy in the morning; * for in thee have I hoped.

Make the way known to me, wherein I should walk: * for I have lifted up my soul to thee.

Deliver me from my enemies, O Lord, to thee have I fled: * teach me to do thy will, for thou art my God.

Thy good spirit shall lead me into the right land: * for thy name's sake, O Lord, thou wilt quicken me in thy justice.

Thou wilt bring my soul out of trouble: * and in thy mercy thou wilt destroy my enemies.

And thou wilt cut off all them that afflict my soul: * for I am thy servant.

During the year, Ant. In thy truth, O Lord, listen unto me.

Paschaltide, Ant. Alleluia, alleluia, alleluia.

Ferial Canticle

Ant. Give ye greatness † to our God. (*P.T.* Alleluia.)

Canticle of Moses [3]

Deut. 32:1-18

Hear, O ye heavens, the things I speak, * let the earth give ear to the words of my mouth.

Let my doctrine gather as the rain, * let my speech distil as the dew,

As a shower upon the herb, † and as drops upon the grass. *

Quasi imber super herbam, †
et quasi stillæ super grámina. *
Quia nomen Dómini invocábo:
Date magnificéntiam Deo nostro. † Dei perfécta sunt ópera, * et
omnes viæ eius iudícia:

Deus fidélis, et absque ulla iníquitate, iustus et rectus. * Peccavérunt ei, et non fílii eius in
sórdibus:

Generátio prava atque pervérsa. * Hǽccine reddis Dómino,
pópule stulte et insípiens?

Numquid non ipse est pater
tuus, * qui possédit te, et fecit, et
creávit te?

Divisio [4]

MEMÉNTO   diérum
antiquórum, * cógita generatiónes síngulas:
Intérroga patrem tuum, et annuntiábit tibi: * maióres tuos, et
dicent tibi.
Quando dividébat Altíssimus
gentes, * quando separábat fílios
Adam,
Constítuit términos populórum
* iuxta númerum filiórum Israel.

Pars autem Dómini, pópulus
eius: * Iacob funículus hæreditátis eius.
Invénit eum in terra desérta, *
in loco horróris, et vastæ solitúdinis:

Because I will invoke the name
of the Lord:

Give ye magnificence to our
God. † The works of God are perfect, * and all his ways are judgments:
God is faithful and without
any iniquity, he is just and right.
* They have sinned against him,
and are none of his children in
their filth:
They are a wicked and perverse
generation. * Is this the return
thou makest to the Lord, O foolish and senseless people?
Is not he thy father, * that hath
possessed thee, and made thee,
and created thee?

Division [4]

REMEMBER the days of old, *
think upon every generation:

Ask thy father, and he will
declare to thee: * thy elders and
they will tell thee.
When the Most High divided
the nations: * when he separated
the sons of Adam,
He appointed the bounds of
people * according to the number
of the children of Israel.
But the Lord's portion is his
people: * Jacob the lot of his inheritance.
He found him in a desert land,
* in a place of horror, and of vast
wilderness:

Saturday - Lauds

Circumdúxit eum, et dócuit: * et custodívit quasi pupíllam óculi sui.

Sicut áquila próvocans ad volándum pullos suos, * et super eos vólitans,

Expándit alas suas, et assúmpsit eum, * atque portávit in húmeris suis.

Dóminus solus dux eius fuit, * et non erat cum eo deus aliénus:

Constítuit eum super excélsam terram, * ut coméderet fructus agrórum:

Ut súgeret mel de petra, * oleúmque de saxo duríssimo;

Butýrum de arménto, et lac de óvibus * cum ádipe agnórum, et aríetum filiórum Basan:

Et hircos cum medúlla trítici, * et sánguinem uvæ bíberet meracíssimum.

Incrassátus est diléctus, ct recalcitrávit: * incrassátus, impinguátus, dilatátus,

Derelíquit Deum factórem suum, * et recéssit a Deo salutári suo.

Provocavérunt eum in diis aliénis, * et in abominatiónibus ad iracúndiam concitavérunt.

Immolavérunt dæmóniis et non Deo, * diis quos ignorábant:

Novi recentésque venérunt, * quos non coluérunt patres eórum:

He led him about, and taught him: * and he kept him as the apple of his eye.

As the eagle enticing her young to fly, * and hovering over them,

He spread his wings, and hath taken him * and carried him on his shoulders.

The Lord alone was his leader: * and there was no strange god with him.

He set him upon high land: * that he might eat the fruits of the fields,

That he might suck honey out of the rock, * and oil out of the hardest stone,

Butter of the herd, and milk of the sheep * with the fat of lambs, and of the rams of the breed of Basan:

And goats with the marrow of wheat, * and might drink the purest blood of the grape.

The beloved grew fat, and kicked: * he grew fat, and thick and gross,

He forsook God who made him, * and departed from God his saviour.

They provoked him by strange gods, * and stirred him up to anger, with their abominations.

They sacrificed to devils and not to God: * to gods whom they knew not:

That were newly come up, * whom their fathers worshipped not.

Saturday - Lauds

Deum qui te génuit dereliquísti, * et oblítus es Dómini creatóris tui.

Ant. Date magnitúdinem Deo nostro. (*T.P.* Allelúia.)

Canticum Festivum

Ant. Osténde nobis, Dómine, † lucem miseratiónum tuárum. (*T.P.* Allelúia.)

Canticum Ecclesiastici [4]

Eccli. 36:1-13

Miserére nostri, Deus ómnium, et réspice nos, * et osténde nobis lucem miseratiónum tuárum:

Et immítte timórem tuum super gentes, * quæ non exquisiérunt te,

Ut cognóscant quia non est Deus nisi tu, * et enárrent magnália tua.

Alleva manum tuam super gentes aliénas, * ut vídeant poténtiam tuam.

Sicut enim in conspéctu eórum sanctificátus es in nobis, * sic in conspéctu nostro magnificáberis in eis,

Ut cognóscant te, sicut et nos cognóvimus, * quóniam non est Deus præter te, Dómine.

Innova signa, et immúta mirabília. * Glorífica manum, et brácchium dextrum.

Excita furórem, et effúnde iram. * Tolle adversárium, et afflíge inimícum.

Thou hast forsaken the God that beget thee, * and hast forgotten the Lord that created thee.

Ant. Give ye greatness to our God. (*P.T.* Alleluia.)

Festal Canticle

Ant. Show us, O Lord † the light of thy mercy. (*P.T.* Alleluia.)

Canticle of Ecclesiasticus [4]

Sir. 36:1-13

Have mercy upon us, O God of all, and behold us, * and shew us the light of thy mercies:

And send thy fear upon the nations, * that have not sought after thee:

That they may know that there is no God beside thee, * and that they may shew forth thy wonders.

Lift up thy hand over the strange nations, * that they may see thy power.

For as thou hast been sanctified in us in their sight, * so thou shalt be magnified among them in our presence,

That they may know thee, as we also have known thee, * that there is no God beside thee, O Lord.

Renew thy signs, and work new miracles. * Glorify thy hand, and thy right arm.

Raise up indignation, and pour out wrath. * Take away the adversary, and crush the enemy.

Saturday - Lauds

Festína tempus, et memént fi- nis, * ut enárrent mirabília tua.

In ira flammæ devorétur qui salvátur: * et qui péssimant plebem tuam, invéniant perditió- nem.

Cóntere caput príncipum in- imicórum, * dicéntium: Non est álius præter nos.

Cóngrega omnes tribus Iacob: † ut cognóscant quia non est Deus nisi tu, * et enárrent magnália tua:

Et hereditábis eos, * sicut ab inítio.

Ant. Osténde nobis, Dómine, lucem miseratiónum tuárum. (*T.P.* Allelúia.)

Ant. In cýmbalis † benesonánti- bus laudáte Deum.
Tempore paschali, Ant. Allelúia, † allelúia, allelúia.

Psalmus 148 [5]

L AUDÁTE Dóminum de cælis: * laudáte eum in excélsis.

Laudáte eum, omnes Ange- li eius: * laudáte eum, omnes virtútes eius.

Laudáte eum, sol et luna: * laudáte eum, omnes stellæ et lu- men.

Laudáte eum, cæli cælórum: * et aquæ omnes, quæ super cælos sunt, laudent nomen Dómini.

Quia ipse dixit, et facta sunt: * ipse mandávit, et creáta sunt.

Hasten the time, and remember the end, * that they may declare thy wonderful works.

Let him that escapeth be con- sumed by the rage of the fire: * and let them perish that oppress thy people.

Crush the head of the princes of the enemies * that say: There is no other beside us.

Gather together all the tribes of Jacob: † that they may know that there is no God besides thee, * and may declare thy great works.

And thou shalt inherit them * as from the beginning.

Ant. Show us, O Lord the light of thy mercy. (*P.T.* Alleluia.)

Ant. Praise God † upon the resounding cymbals.
Paschaltide, Ant. Alleluia, † alleluia, alleluia.

Psalm 148 [5]

P RAISE ye the Lord from the heavens * praise ye him in the high places.

Praise ye him, all his angels: * praise ye him, all his hosts.

Praise ye him, O sun and moon: * praise him, all ye stars and light.

Praise him, ye heavens of heavens: * and let all the waters that are above the heavens, praise the name of the Lord.

Státuit ea in ætérnum, et in sǽculum sǽculi: * præcéptum pósuit, et non prætéribit.

Laudáte Dóminum de terra, * dracónes, et omnes abýssi.

Ignis, grando, nix, glácies, spíritus procellárum: * quæ fáciunt verbum eius:

Montes, et omnes colles: * ligna fructífera, et omnes cedri.

Béstiæ, et univérsa pécora: * serpéntes, et vólucres pennátæ:

Reges terræ, et omnes pópuli: * príncipes, et omnes iúdices terræ.

Iúvenes, et vírgines: † senes cum iunióribus laudent nomen Dómini: * quia exaltátum est nomen eius solíus.

Conféssio eius super cælum et terram: * et exaltávit cornu pópuli sui.

Hymnus ómnibus sanctis eius: * fíliis Israël, pópulo appropinquánti sibi.

Hic non dicitur Gloria Patri.

Psalmus 149 [6]

CANTÁTE Dómino cánticum novum: * laus eius in ecclésia sanctórum.

Lætétur Israël in eo, qui fecit eum: * et fílii Sion exsúltent in rege suo.

Laudent nomen eius in choro: * in týmpano, et psaltério psallant ei:

For he spoke, and they were made: * he commanded, and they were created.

He hath established them for ever, and for ages of ages: * he hath made a decree, and it shall not pass away.

Praise the Lord from the earth, * ye dragons, and all ye deeps:

Fire, hail, snow, ice, stormy winds * which fulfill his word:

Mountains and all hills, * fruitful trees and all cedars:

Beasts and all cattle: * serpents and feathered fowls:

Kings of the earth and all people: * princes and all judges of the earth:

Young men and maidens: † let the old with the younger, praise the name of the Lord: * For his name alone is exalted.

The praise of him is above heaven and earth: * and he hath exalted the horn of his people.

A hymn to all his saints: to the children of Israel, a people approaching him.

Here the Glory be is not said.

Psalm 149 [6]

SING ye to the Lord a new canticle: * let his praise be in the church of the saints.

Let Israel rejoice in him that made him: * and let the children of Sion be joyful in their king.

Let them praise his name in choir: * let them sing to him with the timbrel and the psaltery.

Saturday - Lauds

Quia beneplácitum est Dómino in pópulo suo: * et exaltábit mansuétos in salútem.

Exsultábunt sancti in glória: * lætabúntur in cubílibus suis.

Exaltatiónes Dei in gútture eórum: * et gládii ancípites in mánibus eórum.

Ad faciéndam vindíctam in natiónibus: * increpatiónes in pópulis.

Ad alligándos reges eórum in compédibus: * et nóbiles eórum in mánicis férreis.

Ut fáciant in eis iudícium conscríptum: * glória hæc est ómnibus sanctis eius.

Hic non dicitur Gloria Patri.

Psalmus 150 [7]

LAUDÁTE Dóminum in sanctis eius: * laudáte eum in firmaménto virtútis eius.

Laudáte eum in virtútibus eius: * laudáte eum secúndum multitúdinem magnitúdinis eius.

Laudáte eum in sono tubæ: * laudáte eum in psaltério, et cíthara.

Laudáte eum in týmpano, et choro: * laudáte eum in chordis, et órgano.

Laudáte eum in cýmbalis benesonántibus: † laudáte eum in cýmbalis iubilatiónis: * omnis spíritus laudet Dóminum.

Glória Patri, et Fílio, * et Spirítui Sancto.

For the Lord is well pleased with his people: * and he will exalt the meek unto salvation.

The saints shall rejoice in glory: * they shall be joyful in their beds.

The high praises of God shall be in their mouth: * and two-edged swords in their hands:

To execute vengeance upon the nations, * chastisements among the people:

To bind their kings with fetters, * and their nobles with manacles of iron.

To execute upon them the judgment that is written: * this glory is to all his saints.

Here the Glory be is not said.

Psalm 150 [7]

PRAISE ye the Lord in his holy places: * praise ye him in the firmament of his power.

Praise ye him for his mighty acts: * praise ye him according to the multitude of his greatness.

Praise him with sound of trumpet: * praise him with psaltery and harp.

Praise him with timbrel and choir: * praise him with strings and organs.

Praise him on high sounding cymbals: † praise him on cymbals of joy: * let every spirit praise the Lord.

Glory be to the Father, and to the Son, * and to the Holy Ghost.

Saturday - Lauds

Sicut erat in princípio, et nunc, et semper, * et in sǽcula sæculórum. Amen.

Ant. In cýmbalis benesonántibus laudáte Deum.

Tempore paschali, Ant. Allelúia, allelúia, allelúia.

Capitulum *Rom. 13:12-13*

Nox præcéssit, dies autem appropinquávit. † Abiciámus ergo ópera tenebrárum, et induámur arma lucis. * Sicut in die honéste ambulémus. ℟. Deo grátias.

℟.*br.* Sana ánimam meam, * quia peccávi tibi.

℟. Sana ánimam meam, * quia peccávi tibi.

℣. Ego dixi: Dómine, miserére mei

℟. Quia peccávi tibi.

℣. Glória Patri, et Fílio, * et Spirítui Sancto.

℟. Sana ánimam meam, * quia peccávi tibi.

Hymnus

Auróra iam spargit polum:
Terris dies illábitur:
Lucis resúltat spículum:
Discédat omne lúbricum.

Phantásma noctis décidat:
Mentis reátus súbruat:
Quidquid ténebris hórridum
Nox áttulit culpæ, cadat.

As it was in the beginning, is now, * and ever shall be, world without end. Amen.

Ant. Praise God † upon the resounding cymbals.

Paschaltide, Ant. Alleluia, alleluia, alleluia.

Chapter *Rom. 13:12-13*

THE night is passed, and the day is at hand. Let us therefore cast off the works of darkness, and put on the armour of light. Let us walk honestly, as in the day. ℟. Thanks be to God.

℟.*br.* Heal my soul, * for I have sinned against thee.

℟. Heal my soul, * for I have sinned against thee.

℣. I said: O Lord, be thou merciful to me

℟. For I have sinned against thee.

℣. Glory be to the Father, and to the Son, * and to the Holy Ghost.

℟. Heal my soul, * for I have sinned against thee.

Hymn

The dawn is sprinkling in the east
Its golden shower, as day flows in;
Fast mount the pointed shafts of light:
Farewell to darkness and to sin!

Away, ye midnight phantoms all!
Away, despondence and despair!
Whatever guilt the night has brought,
Now let it vanish into air.

Saturday - Lauds

Et mane illud últimum,
Quod præstolámur cérnui,
In lucem nobis éffluat,
Dum hoc canóre cóncrepat.

Deo Patri sit glória,
Eiúsque soli Fílio,
Cum Spíritu Paráclito,
Et nunc et in perpétuum.
Amen.

℣. Repléti sumus mane misericórdia tua.
℟. Exsultávimus, et delectáti sumus.
Ant. Illumináre, Dómine, † his, qui in ténebris sedent: et dírige pedes nostros in viam pacis, Deus Israël.

In Sabbato B.M.V.
Capitulum   *Eccli. 24:14*

A B inítio et ante sǽcula creáta sum, † et usque ad futúrum sǽculum non désinam, * et in habitatióne sancta coram ipso ministrávi.
℟. Deo grátias.

℟.*br.* Ave María, grátia plena, * Dóminus tecum.
℟. Ave María, grátia plena, * Dóminus tecum.
℣. Benedícta tu in muliéribus, et benedíctus fructus ventris tui.

℟. Dóminus tecum.

So, Lord, when that last morning breaks,
Looking to which we sigh and pray,
O may it to thy minstrels prove
The dawning of a better day.

All laud to God the Father be;
All praise, Eternal Son, to thee;
All glory, as is ever meet,
To God the Holy Paraclete.
Amen.

℣. We are filled in the morning with thy mercy.
℟. And we have rejoiced, and are delighted.
Ant. Enlighten them, O Lord, † that sit in darkness and in the shadow of death, and guide our feet into the way of peace.

On Saturdays of Our Lady
Chapter   *Sir. 24:14*

F ROM the beginning, and before the world, was I created, † and unto the world to come I shall not cease to be, * and in the holy dwelling place I have ministered before him.
℟. Thanks be to God.

℟.*br.* Hail Mary, full of grace, * The Lord is with thee.
℟. Hail Mary, full of grace, * The Lord is with thee.
℣. Blessed art thou among women and blessed is the fruit of thy womb.

℟. The Lord is with thee.

Saturday - Lauds

℣. Glória Patri, et Fílio, * et Spirítui Sancto.

℟. Ave María, grátia plena, * Dóminus tecum.

Hymnus

O gloriósa Dómina,
Excélsa super sídera:
Qui te creávit, próvide
Lactásti sacro úbere.

Quod Heva tristis ábstulit,
Tu reddis almo gérmine:
Intrent ut astra flébiles,
Cæli fenéstra facta es.

Tu Regis alti iánua,
Et porta lucis fúlgida:
Vitam datam per Vírginem,
Gentes redémptæ, pláudite.

Glória tibi Dómine,
Qui natus es de Vírgine,
Cum Patre et Sancto Spíritu,
In sempitérna sǽcula. Amen.

℣. Benedícta tu in muliéribus.

℟. Et benedíctus fructus ventris tui.

Ant. Beáta Dei Génetrix, María, † Virgo perpétua, templum Dómini, sacrárium Spíritus Sancti, sola sine exémplo placuísti Dómino nostro Iesu Christo: ora pro pópulo, intérveni pro clero, intercéde pro devóto femíneo sexu.

℣. Glory be to the Father, and to the Son, * and to the Holy Ghost.

℟. Hail Mary, full of grace, * The Lord is with thee.

Hymn

O glorious lady! throned on high
Above the star-illumined sky;
Thereto ordained, thy bosom lent
To thy Creator nourishment.

Through thy sweet offspring we receive
The bliss once lost through hapless Eve;
And heaven to mortals open lies
Now thou art portal of the skies.

Thou art the door of heaven's high King,
Light's gateway fair and glistering;
Life through a Virgin is restored;
Ye ransomed nations, praise the Lord!

All honour, laud, and glory be,
O Jesu, Virgin-born, to thee;
All glory, as is ever meet,
To Father and to Paraclete. Amen.

℣. Blessed art thou amongst women,

℟. And blessed is the fruit of thy womb.

Ant. O Blessed Mary, † Mother of God, Virgin for ever, temple of the Lord, sanctuary of the Holy Ghost, thou, without any example before thee, didst make thyself well-pleasing in the sight of our Lord Jesus Christ; pray for the people, plead for the clergy, make intercession for all women vowed to God.

Canticum Zachariæ
Luc. 1:68-79

BENEDÍCTUS ✠ Dóminus, Deus Israël: * quia visitávit, et fecit redemptiónem plebis suæ:

Et eréxit cornu salútis nobis: * in domo David, púeri sui.

Sicut locútus est per os sanctórum, * qui a sǽculo sunt, prophetárum eius:

Salútem ex inimícis nostris, * et de manu ómnium, qui odérunt nos.

Ad faciéndam misericórdiam cum pátribus nostris: * et memorári testaménti sui sancti.

Iusiurándum, quod iurávit ad Abraham patrem nostrum, * datúrum se nobis:

Ut sine timóre, de manu inimicórum nostrórum liberáti, * serviámus illi.

In sanctitáte, et iustítia coram ipso, * ómnibus diébus nostris.

Et tu, puer, Prophéta Altíssimi vocáberis: * præíbis enim ante fáciem Dómini, paráre vias eius:

Ad dandam sciéntiam salútis plebi eius: * in remissiónem peccatórum eórum:

Per víscera misericórdiæ Dei nostri: * in quibus visitávit nos, óriens ex alto:

Illumináre his, qui in ténebris, et in umbra mortis sedent: * ad

Canticle of Zacharias
Luke 1:68-79

Blessed be the Lord ✠ God of Israel; * because he hath visited and wrought the redemption of his people:

And hath raised up an horn of salvation to us, * in the house of David his servant:

As he spoke by the mouth of his holy Prophets, * who are from the beginning:

Salvation from our enemies, * and from the hand of all that hate us:

To perform mercy to our fathers, * and to remember his holy testament,

The oath, which he swore to Abraham our father, * that he would grant to us,

That being delivered from the hand of our enemies, * we may serve him without fear,

In holiness and justice before him, * all our days.

And thou, child, shalt be called the prophet of the Highest: * for thou shalt go before the face of the Lord to prepare his ways:

To give knowledge of salvation to his people, * unto the remission of their sins:

Through the bowels of the mercy of our God, * in which the Orient from on high hath visited us:

To enlighten them that sit in darkness, and in the shadow of

Saturday - Lauds

dirigéndos pedes nostros in viam pacis.

Ant. In sanctitáte serviámus Dómino, et liberábit nos ab inimícis nostris.

vel:

Ant. Beáta Dei Génetrix, María, Virgo perpétua, templum Dómini, sacrárium Spíritus Sancti, sola sine exémplo placuísti Dómino nostro Iesu Christo: ora pro pópulo, intérveni pro clero, intercéde pro devóto femíneo sexu.

Kýrie, eléison. Christe, eléison. Kýrie, eléison.

Pater noster, qui es in cælis, sanctificétur nomen tuum: advéniat regnum tuum: fiat volúntas tua, sicut in cælo et in terra. Panem nostrum cotidiánum da nobis hódie: et dimítte nobis débita nostra, sicut et nos dimíttimus debitóribus nostris:

℣. Et ne nos indúcas in tentatiónem:

℟. Sed líbera nos a malo.

℣. Dóminus vobíscum.

℟. Et cum spíritu tuo.

℣. Benedicámus Dómino.

℟. Deo grátias.

℣. Fidélium ánimæ per misericórdiam Dei requiéscant in pace.

℟. Amen.

death: * to direct our feet into the way of peace.

Ant. In holiness let us serve the Lord, and he will deliver us from our enemies.

or:

Ant. O Blessed Mary, Mother of God, Virgin for ever, temple of the Lord, sanctuary of the Holy Ghost, thou, without any example before thee, didst make thyself well-pleasing in the sight of our Lord Jesus Christ; pray for the people, plead for the clergy, make intercession for all women vowed to God.

Lord have mercy upon us, Christ have mercy upon us, Lord have mercy upon us

Our Father, who art in heaven, Hallowed be thy name. Thy kingdom come. Thy will be done on earth as it is in heaven. Give us this day our daily bread. And forgive us our trespasses, as we forgive those who trespass against us.

℣. And lead us not into temptation:

℟. But deliver us from evil.

℣. The Lord be with you.

℟. And with your spirit.

℣. Let us bless the Lord.

℟. Thanks be to God.

℣. May the souls of the faithful, through the mercy of God, rest in peace.

℟. Amen.

Saturday - Lauds   109

℣. Divínum auxílium máneat semper nobíscum.

℟. Et cum frátribus nostris abséntibus. Amen.

℣. May the divine assistance remain with us always.

℟. And with our brothers, who are absent. Amen.

CHAPTERS AND HYMNS FOR LITURGICAL SEASONS

ADVENT

Capitulum   *Isa. 2:3*

VENÍTE, et ascendámus ad montem Dómini, et ad domum Dei Iacob, et docébit nos vias suas, et ambulábimus in sémitis eius: quia de Sion exíbit lex, et verbum Dómini de Ierúsalem.
℞. Deo grátias.

℞.*br.* Veni ad liberándum nos * Dómine Deus virtútum.
℞. Veni ad liberándum nos * Dómine Deus virtútum.
℣. Osténde fáciem tuam et salvi érimus.
℞. Dómine Deus virtútum.
℣. Glória Patri, et Fílio, * et Spirítui Sancto.
℞. Veni ad liberándum nos * Dómine Deus virtútum.

Hymnus

Vox clara ecce íntonat,
Obscúra quæque íncrepat:
Pellántur éminus sómnia;
Ab æthre Christus prómicat.

Chapter   *Is. 2:3*

COME and let us go up to the mountain of the Lord, and to the house of the God of Jacob, and he will teach us his ways, and we will walk in his paths: for the law shall come forth from Sion, and the word of the Lord from Jerusalem.
℞. Thanks be to God.

℞.*br.* Come to my rescue, * O God, Lord of hosts.
℞. Come to my rescue, * O God, Lord of hosts.
℣. show us thy face, and we shall be saved.
℞. O God Lord of hosts.
℣. Glory be to the Father, and to the Son, * and to the Holy Ghost.
℞. Come to my rescue, * O God, Lord of hosts.

Hymn

Hark, a herald voice is calling;
"Christ is nigh," it seems to say;
"Cast away the dreams of darkness,
O ye children of the day."

Advent

Mens iam resúrgat tórpida
Quæ sorde exstat sáucia;
Sidus refúlget iam novum,
Ut tollat omne nóxium.

E sursum Agnus míttitur
Laxáre gratis débitum:
Omnes pro indulgéntia
Vocem demus cum lácrimis,

Secúndo ut cum fúlserit,
Mundúmque horror cínxerit,
Non pro reátu púniat,
Sed nos pius tunc prótegat.

Laus, honor, virtus, glória,
Deo Patri, et Fílio,
Sancto simul Paráclito,
In sæculórum sǽcula.
Amen.

℣. Vox clamántis in desérto:
Paráte viam Dómini.

℟. Rectas fácite sémitas eius.

Startled at the solemn warning,
Let the earth-bound soul arise;
Christ, her sun, all sloth dispelling,
Shines upon the morning skies.

Lo, the Lamb, so long expected,
Comes with pardon down from heaven;
Let us haste, with tears of sorrow,
One and all to be forgiven.

So when next he comes with glory,
Wrapping all the earth in fear,
May he then as our defender
On the clouds of heaven appear.

Honour, glory, virtue, merit,
To the Father and the Son,
With the co-eternal Spirit,
While eternal ages run.
Amen.

℣. A voice of one crying in the wilderness: Prepare the way of the Lord.

℟. Make straight his paths.

LENT

Capitulum Isa. 58:1

CLAMA, ne cesses, quasi tuba exálta vocem tuam, et annúntia pópulo meo scélera eórum, et dómui Iacob peccáta eórum. ℟. Deo grátias.

℟.br. Ipse liberávit me * de láqueo venántium. ℟. Ipse liberávit me * de láqueo venántium. ℣. Et a verbo áspero. ℟. De láqueo venántium.

℣. Glória Patri, et Fílio, * et Spirítui Sancto.

℟. Ipse liberávit me * de láqueo venántium.

Hymnus
Iam Christe sol iustítiæ,
Mentis diéscant ténebræ:
Virtútum ut lux rédeat,
Terris diem cum réparas.

Dans tempus acceptábile,
Et pǽnitens cor tríbue,
Convértat ut benígnitas
Quos longa suffert píetas.

Quiddámque pæniténtiæ
Da ferre, quamvis grávium,
Maióre tuo múnere,
Quo démptio fit críminum.

Chapter Is. 58:1

CRY, cease not, lift up thy voice like a trumpet, and show my people their wicked doings, and the house of Jacob their sins. ℟. Thanks be to God.

℟.br. For he hath delivered me * from the snare of the hunters. ℟. For he hath delivered me * from the snare of the hunters. ℣. And from the sharp word. ℟. from the snare of the hunters.

℣. Glory be to the Father, and to the Son, * and to the Holy Ghost.

℟. For he hath delivered me * from the snare of the hunters.

Hymn
Jesu, salvation's Sun Divine,
Within our inmost bosoms shine,
With light all darkness drive away
And give the world a better day.

Now days of grace with mercy flow,
O Lord, the gift of tears bestow,
To wash our stains in every part,
Whilst heavenly fire consumes the heart.

Rise, crystal tears, from that same source
From whence our sins derive their course;
Nor cease, till hardened hearts relent,
And softened by your streams, repent.

Lent

Dies venit, dies tua,
In qua reflórent ómnia:
Lætémur in hac ad tuam
Per hanc redúcti grátiam.

Te rerum univérsitas,
Clemens, adóret, Trínitas,
Et nos novi per véniam,
Novum canámus cánticum.
Amen.

℣. Angelis suis Deus mandávit de te.
℟. Ut custódiant te in ómnibus viis tuis.

Behold, the happy days return,
The days of joy for them that mourn;
May we of their indulgence share,
And bless the God that grants our prayer.

May heaven and earth aloud proclaim
The Trinity's almighty fame;
And we, restored to grace, rejoice
In newness both of heart and voice.
Amen.

℣. For he hath given his angels charge over thee;
℟. To keep thee in all thy ways.

PASSIONTIDE

Captulum   *Ier. 11:19*

VENÍTE, mittámus lignum in panem eius, et eradámus eum de terra vivéntium, et nomen eius non memorétur ámplius.
℟. Deo grátias.

℟.*br.* Erue a frámea * Deus ánimam meam.
℟. Erue a frámea * Deus ánimam meam
℣. Et de manu canis únicam meam.
℟. Deus ánimam meam.

℟. Erue a frámea * Deus ánimam meam.

Hymnus

Lustris sex qui iam peráctis,
Tempus implens córporis,
Se volénte natus ad hoc,
Passióni déditus,
Agnus in Crucis levátur
Immolándus stípite.

Hic acétum, fel, arúndo,
Sputa, clavi, láncea:
Mite corpus perforátur,
Sanguis, unda prófluit:
Terra, pontus, astra, mundus,
Quo lavántur flúmine!

Crux fidélis, inter omnes
Arbor una nóbilis:

Chapter   *Jer. 11:19*

COME, let us put wood on his bread, and cut him off from the land of the living, and let his name be remembered no more.
℟. Thanks be to God.

℟.*br.* Deliver, * O God, my soul from the sword.
℟. Deliver, * O God, my soul from the sword.
℣. My only one from the hand of the dog.
℟. O God, my soul from the sword.
℟. Deliver, * O God, my soul from the sword.

Hymn

Thirty years among us dwelling,
His appointed time fulfilled,
Born for this, he meets his passion,
For that this he freely willed:
On the cross the Lamb is lifted,
Where his life-blood shall be spilled.

He endured the nails, the spitting,
Vinegar, and spear, and reed;
From that holy body broken
Blood and water forth proceed:
Earth, and stars, and sky, and ocean,
By that flood from stain are free.

Faithful cross! above all other,
One and only noble tree!

Passiontide

Nulla silva talem profert
Fronde, flore, gérmine:
Dulce lignum, dulces clavos,
Dulce pondus sústinet.

Flecte ramos, arbor alta,
Tensa laxa víscera,
Et rigor lentéscat ille,
Quem dedit natívitas:
Ut supérni membra Regis
Miti tendas stípite.

Sola digna tu fuísti
Ferre sæcli prétium,
Atque portum præparáre
Nauta mundo náufrago,
Quem sacer cruor perúnxit,
Fusus Agni córpore.

Glória et honor Deo
Usquequáque altíssimo:
Una Patri, Filíoque,
Inclyto Paráclito:
Cui laus est et potéstas
Per ætérna sæcula.
Amen.

℣. Eripe me de inimícis meis,
Deus meus.
℟. Et ab insurgéntibus in me
líbera me.

None in foliage, none in blossom,
None in fruit thy peers may be;
Sweetest wood and sweetest iron!
Sweetest weight is hung on thee.

Bend thy boughs, O tree of glory!
Thy relaxing sinews bend;
For awhile the ancient rigour,
That thy birth bestowed, suspend;
And the King of heavenly beauty
On thy bosom gently tend!

Thou alone wast counted worthy
This world's ransom to uphold;
For a shipwrecked race preparing
Harbour, like the ark of old;
With the sacred blood anointed
From the smitten Lamb that rolled.

To the Trinity be glory
Everlasting, as is meet;
Equal to the Father, equal
To the Son, and Paraclete:
Trinal Unity, whose praises
All created things repeat.
Amen.

℣. Deliver me from my enemies, O my God.
℟. And defend me from them
that rise up against me.

PASCHALTIDE

Capitulum   *Rom. 6:9-10*

CHRISTUS resúrgens ex mórtuis iam non móritur, mors illi ultra non dominábitur. Quod enim mórtuus est peccáto, mórtuus est semel: quod autem vivit, vivit Deo.

℟. Deo grátias.

℟.*br.* Surréxit Dóminus de sepúlcro, * Allelúia, allelúia.

℟. Surréxit Dóminus de sepúlcro, * Allelúia, allelúia.

℣. Qui pro nobis pepéndit in ligno.

℟. Allelúia, allelúia.

℣. Glória Patri, et Fílio, * et Spirítui Sancto.

℟. Surréxit Dóminus de sepúlcro, * Allelúia, allelúia.

Hymnus

Auróra lucis rútilat,
Cælum láudibus íntonat,
Mundus exsúltans iúbilat,
Gemens inférnus úlulat:

Cum Rex ille fortíssimus,
Mortis confráctis víribus,
Pede concúlcans tártara,
Solvit a pœna míseros.

Chapter   *Rom. 6:9-10*

KNOWING that Christ rising again from the dead, dieth now no more, death shall no more have dominion over him. For in that he died to sin, he died once; but in that he liveth, he liveth unto God.

℟. Thanks be to God.

℟.*br.* The Lord is risen from the sepulchre, * alleluia, alleluia.

℟. The Lord is risen from the sepulchre, * alleluia, alleluia.

℣. Who for us was hanged on the tree.

℟. Alleluia, alleluia.

℣. Glory be to the Father, and to the Son, * and to the Holy Ghost.

℟. The Lord is risen from the sepulchre, * alleluia, alleluia.

Hymn

The morn had spread her crimson rays,
When rang the skies with shouts of praise;
Earth joined the joyful hymn to swell,
That brought despair to vanquished hell.

He comes victorious from the grave,
The Lord omnipotent to save,
And brings with him to light of day
The saints who long imprisoned lay.

Paschaltide

Ille qui clausus lápide
Custodítur sub mílite,
Triúmphans pompa nóbili,
Victor surgit de fúnere.

Solútis iam gemítibus,
Et inférni dolóribus,
Quia surréxit Dóminus,
Respléndens clamat Angelus.

Quǽsumus, Auctor ómnium,
In hoc pascháli gáudio,
Ab omni mortis ímpetu
Tuum defénde pópulum.

Glória tibi Dómine,
Qui surrexísti a mórtuis,
Cum Patre et Sancto Spíritu,
In sempitérna sǽcula.
Amen.

℣. In resurrectióne tua, Christe,
allelúia.
℟. Cæli et terra læténtur, allelúia.

Vain is the cavern's three-fold ward
The stone, the seal, the armed guard;
O death, no more thine arm we fear,
The Victor's tomb is now thy bier.

Let hymns of joy to grief succeed,
We know that Christ is risen indeed;
We hear his white-robed angel's
voice,
And in our risen Lord rejoice.

With Christ we died, with Christ we
rose,
When at the font his name we chose;
Oh, let not sin our robes defile,
And turn to grief the paschal smile.

To Thee Who, dead, again dost live,
All glory, Lord, Thy people give;
All glory, as is ever meet,
To Father and to Paraclete.
Amen.

℣. Christ, in thy resurrection,
alleluia.
℟. Let heaven and earth rejoice, alleluia.